# Training You

*Managing the Corporate Training Function*

K. LEE WATSON

**Published by Oak Tree Systems, Incorporated**

694 Front Street, Lovingston, VA 22949

434.263.6700

http://www.trainingforce.com

http://www.oaktree-systems.com

Date of First Publication:  January 2013

ISBN-13:  978-1478105534

ISBN-10:  1478105534

Oak Tree Systems recognizes the trademark information of companies and products within this work, and recognizes those marks with the appropriate use of capitalization.

**Downloads:**

A number of files referenced in this work are available from the Oak Tree Systems, Inc. DropBox site:  https://www.dropbox.com/sh/z19kxslkjo3hvlg/yzbzGYAycu.   These files are provided as a courtesy, without warranty, expressed or implied, and neither the publisher nor author make any guarantees as to, and assume no responsibility for, their use.

Oak Tree Systems has made a significant effort to ensure accuracy and completeness of the information provided in this publication.  Training is a rapidly-changing field of study; therefore neither Oak Tree Systems nor the authors can guarantee the information provided will remain accurate.   The procedures and methods shown in this publication are based on the most current information available at the time of publication.  This publication is sold and provided without warranty, express or implied.  Oak Tree Systems and the authors make no guarantee as to, and assume no responsibility for, the correctness or applicability of the information contained within.

**Suggestions, Errata, and Questions**

Oak Tree Systems welcomes any feedback readers may have, including suggestions or errata.  Please submit all comments to questions@oaktree-systems.com .

*About Lee Watson*

Lee Watson is currently the Health & Safety Trainer for Environmental, Health, and Safety at Virginia Tech. Since 1992, his primary experience has focused on the role of training in building organizations. A large part of that effort has been creating curricula that integrate technology with traditional methods to improve student outcomes and business performance.

As a technology integrator, Lee was principal author of **MedEMT:  A Learning System for Prehospital Care**. The text was among the first to include a companion CD-ROM with Flash™-based student activities and 3-D animation of medical procedures. He has lectured at the state and national level on the use of technology's role in skills training.

His principal focus lies in teaching a student new skills and abilities in an efficient, common-sense manner. He views instructor development as one of the upcoming challenges as teaching modalities continue to evolve.

A graduate of the Jefferson College of Health Sciences in Roanoke, Virginia, Lee became a Nationally Registered paramedic in 1993. Throughout his career, he has maintained close ties with public safety as both a working professional and instructor. The privilege of caring for patients and educating other public safety providers remain major passions for him. Teaching students skills that literally can mean "life or death" give a true appreciation for the role of quality training. Lee remains active as an emergency responder and mentor, constantly reminding others that they are treating people – not just patients.

Lee resides in Blacksburg, Virginia.

---

*This book is dedicated to educators and training professionals at all levels who contribute to the ongoing notion that the noblest gesture is working together to improve the present condition.*

*To my children and stepchildren… Shelley, Jon, Megan, Blake, Alex, Gabriella, Brooklyn, Emily and Nate:  there is no greater joy than being your father. The greatest training job of all is teaching you everything from counting stars to chasing storms.*

# INTRODUCTION

*Training You* is a book designed for those individuals who take on the challenge of training in the corporate world. There are hundreds of books on the training, so why did I feel the need for yet another?

There wasn't a book out there that told me how to go from being a decent instructor to being in charge of the whole training operation.

This book is full of lists, web links, bullet points, and concepts. A simple Google search on any single concept presented will return a wealth of information. My goal wasn't to cover every single concept in great detail. *Training You* presents a lot of relevant concepts together in a context useful to a training manager – especially the newly appointed one.

I've tied together information on getting students, curricula, technology, environments, and instructors together for a reason. A training manager has to stay focused on these areas and keep them in balance to be successful.

Of special note is the extensive section on learning management systems. I have used systems, purchased systems, and even worked for an outstanding LMS vendor (Oak Tree Systems' *TrainingForce*). I put a lot of thought into writing that section, because working with an LMS is a headache for many training managers.

Training in the trenches is hard work. Some companies overthink it; others underfund it. At the end of the day, training presents an opportunity to work with a lot of great people who put their heart and soul into a business every day. That's why I love it, and you will too.

# TABLE OF CONTENTS

# TRAINING YOU

Managing the corporate training function is a challenge. Today's training manager has roles that cover everything from instructional designer, instructor, administrator, webmaster, information technology specialist, graphic artist... the list is nearly as exhausting as the role. *Training You* is a guide for those tireless individuals tasked with day-to-day management of the corporate training function.

There are literally hundreds of books and web sites dedicated to training, covering everything from adult learning principles to program evaluation. The recipe for a top-notch corporate training program means getting five key ingredients right.

### The Right Students

Getting the right training to the right student is the core mission of a training center. Determining who needs training, on what subjects, and why helps get the right students into training. Without students that are interested and engaged, having all the other pieces won't save a training session.

### The Right Curriculum

The students must be training using a curriculum designed for the job or tasks they are being asked to perform. Simply put, training must be about giving students something new, or allowing them to do something better.

### The Right Technology

Far too many instructors and organizations today rely on technology to make up for poor planning, poor curriculum development and poor instructional techniques. Applying technology in a manner that helps the student achieve the desired outcome is appropriate – replacing a good instructor with a poorly executed online program is not.

### The Right Environment

Students and instructors must have the right environment, including all the tools, training props, and resources necessary. The environment must be realistic and free from distractions.

### The Right Instructors

Selecting and deploying instructors can be a challenging, time consuming element of the Training Manager's job. Instructors that are prepared, motivated and excited about teaching are necessary for training success. Selecting and rewarding the right instructors helps ensure the training budget yields a return on the investment.

# THE CORPORATE YOU-NIVERSITY

The responsibility for training others begins with the responsibility for training "you" – the training manager. A training manager's education is paramount because of the diversity of roles that make up the training function.

Individuals often come to the training manager role by way of a related job, such as instructor or human resources professional. Often, new training managers are well-versed in only one or two roles before assuming responsibility for all of them. Learning, prioritizing, and managing the other roles can be challenging.

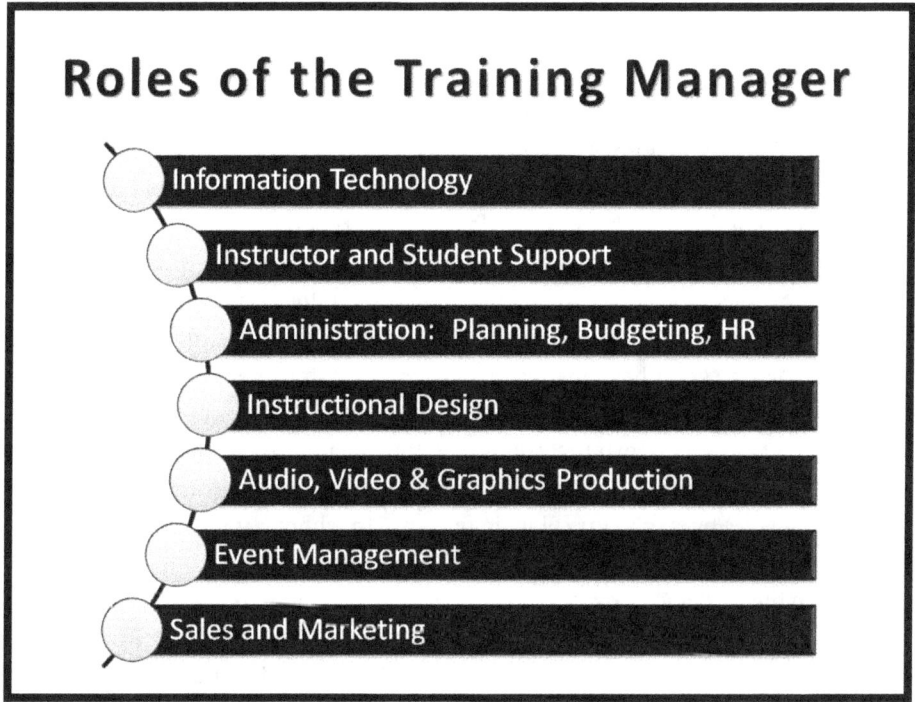

Depending on the resources and structure of the training center, a training manager's role and degree of involvement can vary in each functional area.

## 10 Things to Do First

Being selected to oversee the corporate training function can seem overwhelming even for an experienced training professional.

1. Identify personal weaknesses and limitations with regard to the diverse roles of the training manager. Be honest. Seek mentors, training opportunities or other support in those areas.

2. Be sure the training department's charge from senior management is clearly understood. A detailed report or document is not needed – simply an understanding of what senior management wants the training center to accomplish. Why does the training function exist?

3. Visit each site, each department head and ask "What's your take on training?" Listen to the responses. Be prepared to hear negativity. Accept criticism without accepting responsibility or assigning blame. Even if criticism sounds personal at times, remain impartial and avoid becoming defensive. Take notes.

4. If assuming responsibility for an existing training center, attend several classes. Sit in the back of the class and take notes covering each of the five functional areas: curriculum, technology, environment, instructor, and students.

5. Identify the starting point. Where is the training center at in each of the five areas? Be sure to document information on each functional area. To give an accurate progress report, the training manager must have a good frame of reference.

6. Establish a simple, clearly stated personal vision for the training center. This is different than the formal mission or vision statements; this is a very personal statement of what the training manager feels will define success of the training center. For example, "Develop an in-house instructional staff." Write them down, put a date on the paper, and post it near the computer or telephone. Daily actions should contribute to the long-term fulfillment of these goals.

7. Perform an audit. Identify available resources in each of the functional areas. If the training center has a learning management system, get familiar with the vendor and existing data. Don't restrict the audit to the obvious – include software programs, external contacts, hotel / conference center past contracts, etc. Review existing curricula based on frequency of use and impact on business. Why is this curriculum important? To whom is it important? How does it contribute to the business?

8. Form the first advisory group. From the individuals visited in step three and the people identified as resources in step seven, form an initial advisory group. If taking over a training center from a previous manager, find out if a group exists. If not already invited, ask a couple members of the former group to join as well. Share what's been learned. Let the group brainstorm, and listen carefully to the group dynamics. Use care not to let the group dictate training; the training manager must retain authority and control.

9. Establish a prioritized to-do list. Having a list of higher-priority items that take 3-5 years to develop is normal. Don't overlook items that might have a lesser impact, but can be easily accomplished. The list should also be consistent with the training manager's personal vision. Separate items by functional area, then rate them based on potential short and long-term impact, cost, difficulty, and time required.

10. Develop an outline and timeline using the accumulated information. These are the first steps towards forming the training center's short- and long-term plan.

Establishing credibility as a training manager is a major hurdle. These steps, along with a few completed "to-do" items in each functional area, help build the relationships and credibility needed for the larger-scale projects.

## Understand and Challenge Myths

Training managers are often confronted with misconceptions or myths about corporate training. Will Thalheimer identified and published a list of common myths. Some of the more common include:

- Training is the only way to improve on-the-job performance.
- Showing people the information is sufficient for them to learn.
- Managers/supervisors think training is a low-priority part of their job.
- Students know how to learn.
- Formal training has minimal impact.
- Experienced workers don't need training.
- Developing training is a quick, easy process.
- Training solves every problem.
- People only learn by doing.
- Reading should never be part of training.
- Employees should take all available e-learning classes upon hiring.
- More information and more time equals more learning.
- A large number of training offerings is essential.
- Measure ROI, but not learning.
- Particular behaviors are easy to learn or teach.

(Thalheimer, Myths the Business Side has About Learning, 2009).

Perhaps the most common misconception is that training exists separately from the actual business. This myth is perpetuated because the training function is rarely standardized and training centers exist in many forms. Some are managed as an extension of human resources. Others exist as a separate business unit, such as a training department or corporate university. Larger firms may have multiple training departments – one for Information Technology, one for Safety, etc. An "us (training) vs. them (business)" mentality is common.

Dispelling training myths may not be easy. In many cases they represent years of unchallenged thinking. Some training professionals may have endorsed the myths out of ignorance or laziness. These myths are part of a training manager's reality. Change is a slow process. Pick battles that are important, and that can be won.

---

**Challenge myths using fact and tact.**

---

When a training manager is put in the position of challenging a strongly held misconception, there are two tools needed – fact and tact. Prepare a single-page argument based on fact and research. If there is a financial component, be sure the "bottom line" is clear. Include the opportunity cost. For example, if a training manager spends $1,500 on room seating improvements, that money is not available to fund lunch for an upcoming class in the same room.

When presenting a problem, provide at least three possible options for accomplishing the task. Avoid creating situations that require a strict yes-or-no. Taking the time to present three options helps demonstrate the importance of the issue. Each of the three options should present a different cost / benefit profile. Avoid labeling solutions with numbers or adjectives – instead, use the vendor name or another descriptive noun. Labeling a solution as "Option 1" can be misinterpreted as the preferred choice.

Training managers should use a standardized approach to writing a simple, single-page analysis of the problem and offering solutions. A fact-based proposal should include:

### Problem
State the problem simply, in no more than 2-3 sentences.

### Effects
Explain the impact of the problem in operational, human, and financial terms.

### Solutions
Offer three solutions. Identify the top benefit and drawback for each, along with the cost and impact on the problem's effects.

### Threats
Identify barriers to solving the problem.

Equally important is the manner in which the training manager challenges the myth. Be diplomatic. Do not get emotionally involved – remain tactful and respectful. Present the information and be open to considering options or suggestions. When given the opportunity, offer a clear, reasoned opinion and solution. Anticipate the questions that might be asked, and be prepared to answer them honestly.

Communicating tactfully in the workplace incorporates four basic steps:
- T – Think before speaking
- A – Actively listen to others
- C – Control any emotions
- T – Think and talk positive
  (Anovick, 2010)

There may be occasions where there is disagreement between individuals or groups after presenting an issue for discussion. It is perfectly ok to disagree, but do so without being disagreeable or disrespectful. Present multiple options for resolving an issue. Doing so allows more opportunity for reasoned discussion and compromise. Remember to keep things in perspective. Know which issues can be tabled.

### Prioritize

A training manager must accept that not every issue or misconception presents an emergency requiring immediate action. Some issues, such as those involving the safety of people or property, require urgent attention. For example, impaired or distracted driving would require immediate action by a trucking company.

---

**Know the difference between what MUST change and what SHOULD change.**

---

Other issues may be important but can be addressed less urgently. Approach these through routine mechanisms such as staff meetings. Be prepared, be concise, and be diplomatic. Being able to differentiate between things that must change and things that should change is essential for the training manager to be effective.

Prioritizing issues may not be easy. Accepting that some battles need to be deferred, or even lost, is part of the training manager's life. To prioritize, clearly define the problem and impact. Sort the summarized issues into categories. Training-related issues typically fall into one of four areas:

1. Life and Property Safety Issues
2. Regulatory and Compliance Issues
3. Business Practice Issues
4. Methodology and Best Practice Issues

Within each category, keep issues prioritized by impact and cost. Use opportunities like an annual report to communicate a "top five" issues. A spreadsheet or index card file can be very useful in tracking issues. A sample Issue Tracking sheet is available from the Oak Tree Systems' site: https://www.dropbox.com/sh/z19kxslkjo3hvlg/yzbzGYAycu .

### Case Study: Fire Extinguisher Training

Realistic fire extinguisher training can be fairly complex. A local business is required to use special dry chemical extinguishers throughout the facility. These extinguishers are expensive to recharge (about $75) after each use. They operate differently than water extinguishers. In order to save money on training, the business owner elected to use water extinguishers for employee practice. The myth? "An extinguisher is an extinguisher, a fire is a fire, employees can figure it out." Even though the instructor challenged the myth, management disagreed and left the instructor very little choice. The instructor explained the differences, but all practice was done using the cheaper extinguisher. The total savings to the company during training worked out to about $900. Approximately 60 days after training, a fire occurred. The nearest employee was part of the class, and attempted to put out the fire using a nearby extinguisher. The employee attempted to use the extinguisher as practiced in training, but was unable to do so. The fire remained uncontrolled for several minutes until another employee was able to extinguish the fire. Had the employee been able to control the fire initially, damage would have been minimal.

## Attend Training

Attend training whenever possible – both within the training center and externally. Continuing in the student role also helps a training manager cut through the noise that often surrounds the training industry. Buzzwords and "new ideas" are often promoted by vendors or self-anointed training experts.

Attend external classes that develop knowledge and skills across the various roles of a training manager. Taking online courses on database management might help a training manager communicate more clearly with the learning management system vendor. Attending project or quality management classes at a community college provide a wealth of skills any training manager will find useful.

There are a number of higher education providers that have placed excellent course materials on the web. The Massachusetts Institute of Technology's OpenCourseWare™ Program (http://ocw.mit.edu/index.htm) provides access to information from over 100 higher education institutions. Apple's *iTunes U,* available to Apple users, provides access to another large library of content directly from participating institutions. Much of the content is free and publicly available.

## Avoid Industry Capture

A final concern for the new training manager involves the training industry. Just because someone publishes an article in *Training* does not mean the concept really is the "next best thing." A corporate training manager has to stay abreast of topics that are based on sound principles and support the corporate business model – not every current trend. *Industry capture* refers to a training manager focusing more on the training industry and less on actual training.

Three basic concepts make up the industry capture a training manager should avoid – buzzwords, bad ideas, and self-promotion.

*Popular Mechanics* does a "look back" every so often and the inventions and ideas seem pretty outrageous. Look at the articles about the year 2000, some written as late as the 1970's! Unfortunately, too many training managers follow or promote "the next big thing" and use buzzwords rather than focus on their own organization or creating positive change.

## Buzzwords

Truthfully, the term buzzword isn't that bad. It simply means a new idea or concept that has gathered some attention. When training managers try to keep up with trends (i.e., follow the buzz) there are occasional successes, but more often the exercise simply distracts them from the core job function. Buzzwords create "scope creep" - all training managers have experienced it. Positive change is great. Change without purpose, or without considering how it affects all the stakeholders, can be disastrous.

Vendors, instructors and students are quick to suggest new ideas and changes to training managers. The next time a "buzz" is suggested, go back to basics. Think about what the "buzz" will affect related to job performance. Does the suggestion make the job, task, or program simpler? more profitable? reduce the chance of injury? save time? Generally - be sure it's going to be a positive change before adopting anything. Don't forget, an idea can be scrapped pretty quickly. Don't let personal pride affect decision making – don't keep chasing a bad decision.

## Bad Ideas

Going even beyond buzzwords, some ideas are just bad. Training managers are known for challenging the normal, creating positive change, questioning authority, and all the usual clichés. But training managers also have to be able to identify and eliminate ideas that are bad. So what makes something a bad idea? Bad ideas are:

- Something that may be appropriate for one company but does not apply or requires changes to be applied effectively, for the current situation.
- A specific course of action that should be easily supported by research, that is only supported by nonspecific statements.
- Actions suggested with blindness to past failures or successes. An idea or concept that has been unsuccessful in the past, without solid data on why it should be expected to succeed now, is a bad idea. Overemphasizing successes can lead you down the wrong road as well.
- Ideas communicated ineffectively. Even the best idea comes across as a bad idea if not communicated clearly.

## Self-Promotion

Training sessions present a unique environment. Training managers, as well as any instructor or staff member, must disclose any real or perceived conflicts of interest. Training managers are in place to support the growth and development of the company. While there is some latitude for scholarly activity, a training manager should not engage in self-promotion.

Training managers also have to ensure others respect the purpose of the training center. Some instructors and students may be exceptionally knowledgeable and gifted, yet have their own agenda.  One highly gifted OSHA trainer was known for using sessions on personal protective equipment to market a line of safety boots and gloves to students.

A conflict of interest doesn't have to be a formal relationship with a vendor. A conflict of interest exists, at the most basic level, when an individual stands to gain something of value by advancing a specific belief of position.

Managing conflicts can be simple, as long as they are known.

- Include conflict disclosure statements as part of any application or selection process for employees or instructors.
- Ask individuals with a potential conflict to refrain from any discussion or decision-making involving the conflict.
- Ensure that classes present multiple options and allow students to select the most appropriate for their application.
- Involve a 3rd party to lead discussions or present an objective assessment.
- Defer to any applicable Code of Ethics.  Remember that some individuals (politicians, lawyers, and health care professionals among others) may be legally required to make disclosures if a conflict exists.

### The Learning and Development Industry

Not all ideas and information is bad. A training manager should definitely read a variety of publications and blogs. The trick is to pick and choose those ideas that have value to the specific needs of the training center and business.

#### The Top 5 Resources for Training Managers

- American Society of Training & Development (http://www.astd.org/)
  ASTD is the largest professional training organization out there. Membership is a bit pricey, but there's a ton of information available for free on their web site.
- *Employee Training and Development*, 5th Edition by Raymond A. Noe.
  For corporate training managers, this text covers a wealth of information.
- *Training* (http://www.trainingmag.com/)
  *Training* magazine (and it's associated web site) is more of a trade publication. This is a great resource for identifying vendors.
- Will Thalheimer's *Will at Work Learning* (http://www.willatworklearning.com/).
  Outstanding blog, focusing on results-oriented training.  This should be in every training manager's "Favorites" list.
- *Workforce Online* (http://www.workforceonline.com/)
  A general-purpose website that provides a wealth of information and articles on general human resources topics, including workforce training.

# THE RIGHT STUDENTS

Students are the lifeblood of a training organization.  Getting the right students to the right class with the right attitude involves a number of considerations.

- Identifying who needs training
- Managing skills and competencies
- Marketing training
- Motivating students

Students have to be a constant consideration in training.  To keep students returning to classes, the training center must deliver a quality product.

## Identifying Who Needs Training

Getting the right students involved in a training class begins with understanding who needs training, on what topics, and how often. There are literally hundreds of approaches to answering these questions. Three basic approaches can provide a training manager with options for developing initial lists of training needs.

### The 3-Question Task Test

Training managers can use a very simple test to identify high-priority training needs:

1. Importance:  Is the skill one that the employee must get right the first time?
2. Frequency:  Is the skill one that the employee will perform infrequently?
3. Difficulty:  Is the skill technically complex?

Answering yes to any one of these questions indicates training should be a critical component.  For example, take an employee's use of a portable fire extinguisher.  An employee performs the task infrequently but when performed, the skill must be done correctly.  Answering yes to more than one question elevates the training's priority. (Noe, 2010).

### Training Triggers

There are a number of triggers that provide a reason to train:

- Changes to legislative or regulatory requirements
- A lack of basic skills
- Poor performance
- New technologies
- New products or services
- New employees / job changes
- Need to increase performance

- Performance or skills gaps

## The Needs Assessment

A needs assessment is more comprehensive than the 3-Question Task Test or Trainig Triggers. A needs assessment is part of the formal instructional design process. A formal needs assessment helps a training manager meet the following goals:

- Ensure training is not being used to solve a performance problem.
- Identify the correct content, methods and outcomes for training.
- Identify basic prerequisites and skills needed to be successful in training.
- Correlate training activity with expected goals and business strategy. (Noe, 2010)

A formal needs assessment consists of three basic parts: an organizational analysis, a person analysis, and a task analysis.

### *Organizational Analysis*

An organizational analysis begins with a look at the company's strategic direction. The training needed so that a company can conduct operations is the foundation of the organizational analysis. The organization analysis also helps show the types of training an organization will support.

- What training is needed to meet short and long-term strategic initiatives?
- What training programs will employees, managers, vendors, suppliers, and customers support?
- What types of training will be perceived as presenting an opportunity or being a reward?
- Does the company have institutional knowledge to develop the necessary training programs?
- What company resources are available to support training?

### *Person Analysis*

Identify factors that are needed for a student to be successful in the training itself:

- What basic skills do students need to participate in training, such as reading level?
- Can students understand the task and how it is performed?
- Do students understand the situational factors in performing the task?
- Will students have the opportunity to perform the skill?
- Can students relate the training to job performance?
- Are feedback mechanisms available after training?

### *Task Analysis*

The final part of the formal needs assessment process is a task analysis. The task analysis is a breakdown of the tasks a person performs as part of the job. The initial tasks can come from a job description, direct observation of the job, or from the manager or supervisor.

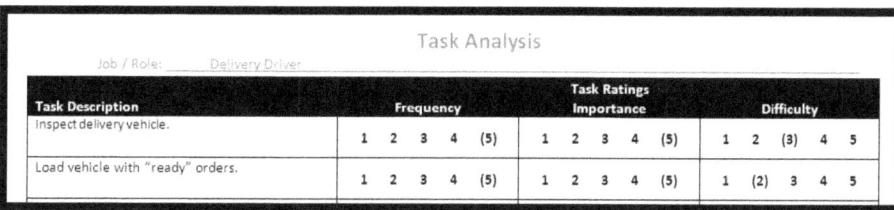

In short, the task analysis helps answer a third set of questions:

- What tasks are truly critical to business operations?
- What tasks are the most difficult?
- What tasks are shared among multiple jobs or roles?
- Are there jobs or roles that ask employees to perform multiple critical tasks?

*Putting the Needs Assessment Together*

A needs assessment can be time-consuming to develop, but is potentially the best with regard to the amount of information available to the training manager. An organizational analysis answers the most basic question – does the company want to devote time and money to training? If so, on what issues? The information from the person analysis might be used to develop training prerequisites and. Understanding what happens at the task level brings worker competency into the equation.

Once information from the three elements is available, the training manager can then start identifying training opportunities. Much of the corporate training function centers around building competency in core skills.

## Managing Certifications, Skills and Competencies

Ensuring employees remain competent at job skills is a constant challenge. Employees love certificates and certifications; many a cube wall is dedicated to framed or push-pinned testaments of activity. In corporate environments, almost every training activity comes with a certificate. Most people view certificates as a testament to having "finished" something. Is there a relationship between certificates or certification and competency?

### What's the Difference?

Certificates say little about the individual student's skill level as it pertains to the workplace. Think about a college degree or a driver's license. Consider the training of local firefighters and paramedics. Does an 18-year-old, freshly licensed driver have the same level of skill as a driver with 30,000 miles behind the wheel? Certificates and certifications actually represent the beginning of something. Define each term in relation to training and the workplace:

*Certification*

The individual has acquired specific knowledge, skills and abilities, measured at a specific moment in time, as determined by the training or instructional staff.

*Skill ( Competency )*

A skill is simply a task to perform. Competency is an individual's demonstration, over a period of time, proper application of knowledge and ability in a real-world environment.

*Track Skills & Competency*

In order to base manage competency using training, performance must be tracked. Skills necessary for each employee are normally reflected on a job description and should mirror any skills identified in a task analysis. These skills are reviewed with employees infrequently at best - usually as part of a "360-degree review" or employee evaluation.

Reviewing skill performance infrequently, or relying solely on certification, presents two problems. First, employees should receive frequent feedback. Feedback can be positive or corrective, and it needs to be ongoing, specific, and relevant. Second, there is typically a huge gap between job expectations and job descriptions. Nearly 80% of participants in a recent study related moderate to high levels of discrepancy between their job's description and actual job expectations. (Barbouletos, 2011).

Employers are concerned with maximizing performance in an employee's current job or position. Really good companies are concerned with grooming employees for future roles. That's where training managers need to draw a distinction. The definitions above provides a good break point:

- Use ongoing skill and competency evaluation to monitor performance in the current job.
- Use the acquisition of certifications (i.e., additional knowledge, skills and abilities) to prepare an employee for a future job or responsibility.

Monitoring and improving employee performance of job skills is the priority. Helping employees is important, but secondary. Both are within the scope of the training manager.

Skill and competency tracking provides a bridge between human resources, training managers, supervisors and the workforce. A learning management system should be able to print beautiful certificates, but more importantly - can a manager observe an employee in the work environment and record relevant feedback using a mobile device?

*Case Study: Paramedics, Certification & Competency*

The paramedics that arrive on an ambulance must be certified or licensed (usually a state function). Certifications are earned through knowledge and skills testing after hundreds of hours of training. This means that on the date tested, the paramedic demonstrated the knowledge, skills, and abilities necessary to be a paramedic.  There are specific requirements that must be met to renew each certification.  Because the role of the paramedic is vital to the daily functioning of the 911 system, most agencies monitor competency of each and every provider frequently.  This monitoring takes many forms: demonstrating skills in laboratory training sessions; reviewing documentation from 911 calls; observation by a field training officer; and rotations in clinical environments.  The certification is important, but competency is what both the employer and the public demand.

## Bridging Gaps

Monitoring skill and competency in the workforce provides a wealth of information to the training center.  There are a number of data points that can be beneficial.

- Skills performance in relation to expected levels by employee segments.
- Individual employee performance of a single skill.
- Individual employee performance over multiple skills.
- Skill compliance monitoring - required versus actually acquired.
- Amount of time to reach a specific skill level.
- Relationship between similar skills and employee performance level

---

**Use gap analysis to establish training priorities.**

---

A skills gap analysis is a way of looking at the data that's been captured.  A skills gap analysis shows the skill, identifies the current performance level, and compares it to the desired performance level.  Consider problems throughout the process.

- Why does the actual performance deviate from expected?
- Is there a problem with the way the skill has been taught?
- Is there a problem with how the skill is being observed or scored by the evaluator?
- Why is the individual having trouble performing at the desired level?

A *skills gap* is the difference between an employee's actual and desired performance level.  A *performance gap* is the difference within a group of employees – the difference between the most capable and least capable personnel.

Once an area is identified where individual or group performance is beneath expectations, the training manager can schedule programs and direct resources in an appropriate manner.

---

**A training manager can make rapid gains by focusing on areas where the performance gap is the widest.**

---

Certificates are a great way to recognize participation in training and academic achievement. To the training manager, the link between training and job performance is a measure of training success or failure.

## Marketing Training

Many corporate training organizations spend the majority of time and effort creating and delivering course materials. "Each employee must complete two classes annually" statements are included in many performance appraisals. Marketing training to a captive workforce may seem odd at first. Good marketing can increase enrollment of voluntary programs, improve perception of training, and improve transfer of training.

Training managers should have a relationship with the corporate marketing team. Ideally, have a marketing professional assigned to support training marketing efforts. Consistency of branding with corporate efforts is very important.

### Create a Marketing Plan

Does the training center have a marketing plan? It should. Even if training is provided only to employees at no charge a marketing plan is essential. Marketers use a variety of skills and tools. Package design, placement, branding, advertising and image are all elements. Some basic questions can help create a basic plan:

1. What is the training center's product? What *exactly* is being marketed?
2. What is the market or audience? What are the characteristics of these employees?
3. What is the competition; that is – what can keep the training product from being successful?
4. Outline strategies to market the product to the audience.
5. Define metrics to measure success of the marketing plan.

### Develop Training as a Brand

Most companies spend significant amounts of money, time and effort on developing the corporate brand. Some brands become so synonymous with a product, all similar products become known by the brand (such as Kleenex, Band-Aid, Scotch tape).

Training should have an identity and brand, even if only a variation of the corporate brand. Certain steps taken in defining and managing the training brand can be leveraged in other areas of training. For example, defining the logo and style contributes to the look and feel of training materials. If corporate brand or marketing has a style guide, mirror that effort.

The concept of developing training as a brand is so important the FIA Institute for Motor Sport Safety and Sustainability (http://www.fiainstitute.com/) actually includes branding as an element of their accreditation of training programs. "The programme has its own identity, including logo, micro-website, apparel, colour schemes, etc." (FIA Institute for Motor Sport Safety and Sustainability, 2012).

Having a clearly defined brand can be a valuable tool. For example, instructors that show up wearing embroidered button-down shirts or dress attire with matching lapel pins can send a strong image of professionalism.

## Create Personal and Professional Value

One of the ideal ways to motivate students is to explicitly create personal or professional value.

### *"What's in this for me?"*

Even though the question seems self-indulgent, it's a question that training managers and instructors need to answer during training. Today's society places great value on time; people seem to have more things to do and less time to do them each passing year. When asking an employee to attend training, the company is asking for an additional chunk of that time.

Even if personnel are attending as part of their normal work schedule, while in training work is either accumulating or someone is doing the job. Ensuring that programs have value to students is a critical function of training. Communicating that value to potential students is an essential component of both marketing and motivating.

Recognizing the difference between personal and professional value is important, too. Take advantage of opportunities to market to both. Training in Six Sigma or as a project management professional (PMP) provide a real benefit to the company, but also benefit the student in the event they seek a promotion or explore other opportunities.

### *Incentives and Recognition*

Two words: Food and Freebies. Students are acutely aware of the economy, so simple gestures like beverages and snacks are very important. Giveaways have taken on new life, as well – but avoid gimmicky corporate stuff. Useful or fun items get a lot of attention. Offer up prizes: a PlayStation 3, a gift card of sufficient value to cover a meal for 2-4 people, a quality golf shirt or hat with the training brand. Giving away low-value gift cards from obscure places or trinkets from the corporate supply closet can have a negative impact. A classic bad example: giving an engraved pewter business card holder to students, when half the attendees were staff employees without business cards.

Recognition is important. Some ways to gain a lot of value, with minimal effort:

- Be sure each attendee gets an appropriate certificate, available through the learning management system. A little effort in design makes a huge difference in how the certificate is received.
- Take photos. E-mail a class photo to each participant with a "thank you" from the instructor or staff member.
- Post photos to the learning management system or corporate intranet site.

- A hand-written note from a member of senior management to an individual in the class, for a specific contribution.

## Communicate Responsibly

Marketing does not mean blasting the entire corporate address book with training e-mails mercilessly. Communications should be an extension of the training brand and the overall marketing plan. The marketing plan should contain a simple calendar, outlining training-related communications.

### E-Mails

Every e-mail sent by the training center must have value for the recipient. Target e-mails to appropriate parties – such as registered students or students with expiring certifications. Use the learning management system's capabilities to create personalized, targeted e-mails.

Use proper e-mail etiquette. Send messages at appropriate times. Allow individuals to opt-out of e-mails that aren't specific to their individual training activity. E-mail should be sent using a common template from a person within the training department, not a "catchall" e-mail account.

### Web Presence

A training center's web presence can be a source of information, engagement, and interaction with the student population. Often, the training center's web page is an extension of the learning management system. A web page should allow individuals to easily identify training of value and register. Even when approval is required by another party such as a manager or staff member, students should be able to initiate the registration process. Solicit ideas for new course offerings and class requests.

### Marketing

Creating a marketing plan for the training center can pay huge dividends. Learners arrive more engaged, because they already know why the topic is of value. Consistency and support of corporate branding efforts makes the training center appear more valuable in the "big picture" as well. Most learning management systems have automated tools for marketing – using them helps improve return on that investment. Marketing doesn't have to be complicated – work with corporate resources, create a simple plan, and execute it well.

## Motivating Students

Motivation can be a challenge, especially for corporate training managers that deal primarily with regulatory compliance training. Students may be motivated to attend training for a variety of reasons – a desire for personal growth, financial incentives, or simply to meet a job requirement. Understanding the motivation for a student to attend training is part of understanding the training audience.

The responsibility for keeping a student motivated shifts to the training manager and instructor once a student enters the training environment. There are four basic elements of student motivation that a training manager and instructors can build upon:

- Build common ground.
- Ensure knowledge is used.
- Recognize individuals, build a team.
- Maximize impact.

To understand motivation, instructors can draw from the experience of professional athletic coaches.

### Build Common Ground.

Athletic coaches work in environments where the current season or game is what's important. A coach's past championships are largely irrelevant to the team at hand. In training, management often tends to take the opposite approach. Training centers routinely view what's been done by an instructor in the past (degrees, publications, presentations) as sufficient to build credibility with the students. Sometimes this is a disservice to the students. Students want and need an instructor that shares common ground with them. When a student sees an instructor with common ground, and the instructor is passionate about the subject matter – it is far easier to create a passion for the topic in the student.

Understanding the audience is a key to finding common ground and subsequently, motivation. Although training staff must retain the authority and control associated with being an educator, simply using inclusive language such as "we" and "us" makes a difference. The common ground doesn't have to be relevant to the subject matter; it can be a shared experience, a symbol, or organizational tradition.

**The creative use of symbols and traditions provide student motivation.**

Shared experiences or traditions present a great motivational opportunity. Sports coaches are extremely creative, using a wide variety of symbols and traditions.

*Case Study: Virginia Tech's Lunch Pail Defense*
The Virginia Tech football team's defensive coach uses a beat-up lunch pail as a symbol of the team's blue collar attitude and work ethic. The lunch pail is awarded to the defensive player who works hardest each week - not always the player with the best on-field performance. The pail carries a mission statement for the year - signed by every member of the defensive unit. The lunch pail is not just about individual performance, it represents the team. The team also places bits of grass from key road wins in the pail as a reminder of what good teamwork can accomplish.

### Ensure knowledge is used.

Trainers should ensure a student's knowledge, skills and abilities are put to use at every opportunity. An instructor cannot spend two hours teaching safety, only to have a subsequent instructor allow students to use unsafe practices during a skills session. The training staff should reinforce each other's efforts frequently to achieve a common, realistic goal. Especially during skills training sessions, an instructor more accurately resembles a sports coach than an academic lecturer.

For example, every coach and assistant uses the same playbook and language. Coaches constantly move up and down the slopes of the same knowledge pyramid familiar to training professionals, transitioning between improving finite elements of a single skill and coaching the play of the entire team.

When an individual has issues at one level the instructor must be willing to go back to the level at which the mistake occurred, correct the mistake, and bring the student back up to speed. Doing so requires consistency between educators and curricula. Motivation involves helping the student understand how the individual bits and pieces actually get used to achieve the larger outcome.

### Recognize individuals, build a team.

Every team has star players, a supporting cast, and substitutes. Part of a coaching staff's responsibility is figuring out how each individual fits into the overall team while minimizing the performance gap. The performance gap is different from skills gap. A skills gap relates to a specific individuals' performance against expectations. The performance gap relates to a group of individuals performing the same skill. The performance gap can be defined as the difference in skill performance between the most proficient and least proficient individuals. Motivation is a balancing act; instructors must get lesser achievers to improve performance, while not allowing higher achievers to get bored. The overall goal is to close the performance gap (i.e., so the 3rd string backup performs in a manner as close to the starter as possible).

So how can instructors recognize individuals? Let the stars take mentoring roles with mid-range students (under a watchful eye, of course). Doing so allows trainers more time to build performance in students having deeper challenges. Success at a task provides motivation. Instructors should provide frequent feedback. Use small but constant statements to help individuals feel successful. Not every student will be a stellar achiever, and there should always be corrective feedback. Allow students to enjoy success at whatever level they achieve.

Motivation at the team level also involves flexibility. Allow students to explore aspects of skills or tasks where strict compliance isn't necessary. Recognize any efforts that result in an improved process. A student's suggestion being implemented or added to the curriculum is a huge motivator not only for the single student, but the entire team.

## Maximize Impact.

Motivation extends beyond a single moment. What's taught at the knowledge level in the classroom works best when students have the ability to go apply that knowledge in a timely fashion. The training manager and instructors need to give students tools so that they can acquire the skill, not put up road blocks to success. All too frequently, the training staff will try to accomplish too much in one session, don't have appropriate resources, or fail to provide opportunities to apply knowledge. Creating a learning opportunity the student won't forget.

When motivating students, help them understand that they can - and will - have a real impact. During training sessions, have previous students discuss how training had an impact on specific situations. Success provides reassurance and motivation. When a previous student has success in applying the tools learned in class, recognize the effort.

## Motivation as an Instructor Responsibility

Instructors are taught early on about Maslow's Hierarchy of Needs. In essence, Maslow proposed that human motivation is based on people seeking fulfillment and change through personal growth. It's the basic responsibility of an instructor to show a student how specific material meets his or her need to grow as a person. How the instructor meets that responsibility plays a huge role in how motivated the student becomes. Many instructors have trouble bridging Maslow's work to real instructional practice. Consider how a parent provides motivation to children. Building a connection and sharing a passion for the topic with students can be a powerful instructional tool.

# THE RIGHT CURRICULUM

Regardless of what type of training is being provided, the best students, instructors and technology cannot make up for an inconsistent, dated, or poorly produced curriculum. There are six fundamental concepts critical to developing or acquiring the right curriculum.

- Focus on the Outcome
- Use Peer Review / Development Groups
- Understand the Audience
- Provide Good Information
- Use Pilot Programs
- Evaluate and Update Consistently

## Focus on the Outcome

The first thing that should come to mind when considering building or adopting a curriculum is the last thing produced by the curriculum – the student. What skill does the student gain or refine during this activity? This used to be called the "terminal objective"; the current phrase is student learning outcome.

At the end of the training day students need to come away with something they can put into use. There are thousands of excellent training programs out there delivering knowledge – but the best programs always allow a student to "do" something new, or "do" something better. Knowledge is only useful if the brain that stores it puts it to good use.

The training center must always keep the students in mind. If training managers want to keep students returning to class, the training organization must deliver a quality product. This is especially true for training managers operating a for-profit training center.

When training managers first start the curriculum evaluation or design process, there are two crucial questions that must be answered:

- What does the organization expect the student to be able do when they complete the program?
- How does the student being able to do the new or refined thing benefit the organization or company?

### Student Learning Outcomes

For years many educators didn't really pay much attention to the slide that often appeared right after the title slide. The slide, or even worse – slides, that listed

"Objectives". Almost every trainer or educator will admit to simply disregarding a review of the objectives in one or more classes.

Outcomes are a throwback. They focus on a simple concept – how the student behaves after the training program. For example, a classical objective might be written as: "Upon completion of this class, the student will be able to identify the emergency stop button." It's specific, measurable, and attainable. Everyone probably remembers those basic rules of objective writing. Does the company or instructor really want the student to simply identify the switch?

What the instructor really wants is for the student to understand why the switch is there, be able to locate and press the button, and make correct situational decisions about when the button should be used. Although student learning outcomes have been a staple of the academic world for the past few years, corporate instructional design has been a bit slower.

If the difference is elusive, consider that George Carlin once said "People add words to make things sound more important than they really are." If the formal term is *student learning outcome* sounds too academic, the shortened form "outcome" is acceptable.

### *Objectives and Outcomes*

One instructor development textbook lists the following as an objective: "Identify positive and negative instructor characteristics." No doubt, most experienced training managers can identify good and bad behaviors in instructors. But what was the author of the book really trying to get the instructor to *do*? The author is actually trying to convince the reader to be a "good" instructor instead of a "bad" one. The goal is not only to identify behaviors; the goal is to have instructors conduct themselves properly. So what could the author or curriculum designer have used to better describe the student's outcome?

One problem with outcome-based education is that with certain programs, evaluating whether a student met the outcome can be more difficult. Evaluating the behavior of new instructors in the classroom is far more time consuming and challenging than grading a simple knowledge examination. Despite the challenges, many existing evaluation tools remain both usable and relevant. Students must still recognize the inappropriate characteristics. With the switch to outcomes, many existing tools simply become part of an overall assessment of the student's ability.

The best curricula take a higher-level view of competency and performance. When training paramedics and emergency medical technicians (EMTs), a typical instructor always asks one final question before signing off on the student: Can this candidate take care of a member of my family in an emergency?

### Why Are Outcomes Good Instructional Design?

Transitioning from traditional objectives to outcomes is a beneficial process for the training center.

#### Controversy

The transition process from objectives to outcomes presents a great opportunity to discuss what is happening in training. Why are things being done a specific way? Is there a better way?

#### Simplicity

The move allows a training center to combine multiple learning objectives into a single, simpler outcome once the focus is on the actual desired end result.

#### Flexibility

The use of outcomes often provides more freedom for instructional designers and instructors. Multiple viewpoints or methodologies can be used to reach the same outcome, which is useful when the student population is diverse.

#### Accountability

Both students and instructors clearly understand the expected result. Students can more clearly understand what they should learn from each instructor.

#### Assessments

Outcomes clearly define what the training center should assess in each student. Outcomes allow assessment at a higher level than objectives.

#### Relevance

By focusing on the end result, students are required to demonstrate mastery at a higher level than simple motor skills or knowledge recall. Students must be able to pull information from across their knowledge and skill base and apply different elements as required by the situation.

### Writing Effective Outcomes

In the simplest form, outcomes express what a student should be able to do. Just like objectives, outcomes should be measurable and attainable. Here's a simple A-B-C-D-E framework for writing good outcomes:

#### A. Antecedent

Antecedents set conditions, materials, environments, or other variables needed. An antecedent isn't always necessary; in many situations it may be implied. Ask if the student can reach the outcome without clarification or other information. Limit the amount of information provided to what is absolutely critical.

#### B. Bloom

Bloom's taxonomy is still the best source for selecting an appropriate verb for the outcome. The higher-order verbs found in analysis, synthesis and evaluation are more accurate when preparing outcomes. Use only verbs that result in a measurable outcome. Even though Bloom is a foundation of instructional design, some verbs are vague and not easily measured.

## C. Criteria

Criteria are necessary when quantity, quality, timing and other components of evaluation are elements of the outcome. Criteria are normally found when a very specific, important outcome is defined.

## D. Draft

Prepare a draft outcome statement. Keep the basics in mind. What does the student need? What actions are expected, and what should the action result in? Are the results specific and measurable? Above all, keep outcomes relevant and simple. Don't overthink. Don't state the obvious. If asking someone to stripe a football field, leading the outcome with "given a grass field of sufficient size" probably isn't necessary.

## E. Evaluate

Look at the outcome after the draft is written. Evaluate where it fits in the individual class and the overall training program. Does the outcome align neatly with others? Outcomes can be specified at the overall program or course level, at the class level, and at the actual session level. The more diligently outcomes are employed at each level, the stronger the overall program will become. (Tallahassee Community College, 2012)

## Instructional Design and Outcomes

Instructional design teaches that a training organization should constantly evaluate training; the same goes for outcomes. Evaluate how students perform during assessments. Ask about the correlation between instruction and the outcome as part of the class evaluation tool. Evaluate the outcome against the job performance as part of the curriculum review.

Student learning outcomes represent a positive change for students, instructional design team members, and instructors. Increased flexibility of design and instruction, coupled with a simpler presentation of the desired result help students succeed.

When considering using a curriculum that is already developed using traditional chapter-by-chapter objectives, consider adapting the materials. Take the time to compile a list of the published objectives and write student learning outcomes as the student and instructor materials are evaluated. If the training center finds it hard to correlate the materials to the outcomes needed, that should be a red flag.

If developing training material within the training organization, use student learning outcomes as a road map to the content. After development, have other stakeholders or subject matter experts review the material and identify content that cannot be clearly tied to a student learning outcome. Consider adding or modifying outcomes if the extra content really needs to be included, or deleting the content if it isn't critical. Remember that a student is committing time to attend a training program, and time is valuable to everyone. Show respect for that commitment by cutting out extraneous or irrelevant content.

## Use Peer Review / Development Groups

One of the easiest ways to ensure the quality of a curriculum's content is to form a peer review or development group. Publishers rely on these types of groups extensively, and they do so for a reason. Feedback, especially in the early stages of a project, can be extremely valuable. As the project matures, these groups can provide great insight into the student and instructor experience.

Once a training need is identified, put together a group to serve as a resource for the project. As an alternative, a training organization can form a single trusted group to provide feedback on multiple training projects, or even serve as an unofficial "board of directors". Allow the group to meet on a set schedule. Involving individuals outside the training department, or even from outside the company can build credibility for the finished product.

Although these groups are extremely valuable, be sure that the training organization retains control of the finished training project. Intellectual property rights are valuable, so consult with legal counsel and set firm guidelines related to the group. Formal agreements may be appropriate in some situations where sensitive information or trade secrets are being discussed.

The group's purpose should be the free and open exchange of ideas related to the moderator's agenda, or their assignments.

Review the business or training need that is driving the project and set parameters for the group. In some cases the moderator may choose to make assignments for specific tasks, or simply set an agenda. Ensure there is a timeline for the group's involvement. Even with the best participants, sometimes meetings can take unexpected turns or have "off" days. Show respect for the group's time by keeping the meetings on-task and on-schedule.

Members of the group can be internal or external, but should be diverse enough to give honest feedback. Even if there are no active projects, sometimes simply brainstorming and talking about the current state of existing training programs can lead to discussion and positive change. Ask questions, have them review content and make suggestions.

Development groups often work by teleconference or web-based meeting. Face-to-face meetings are not always critical and can be costly. Use technology to keep costs down. Document-sharing sites such as Acrobat.Com, Microsoft Office Live, or Google Docs can allow multiple users to edit a document. That type of flexibility is valuable and can allow everyone to get the most value from the actual meeting. These web applications also allow group members to work on projects at their leisure. For corporate users, be sure the use of such sites conforms to Information Technology (IT) policy, or work with the IT staff to provide an alternative solution.

Once the outcome of the program is established, the remaining elements of the curriculum can be evaluated or developed.

## Understand the Audience

Understanding the audience is a significant challenge for any curriculum manager or content developer faces.  Consider three key things with any audience:

- To whom am I speaking?
- What do I want them to know, do, or believe as a result of this session?
- What is the most effective way of composing and communicating the information to accomplish that with this group?

The instructor must be able to establish common ground with the audience.  Good instructors can do this quickly and effectively because they frequently share past similar experiences. Sharing a quick story, especially if it demonstrates a lesson learned the hard way, can help the audience identify with the instructor as a person, not just a speaker.  Good curricula allow time and help the instructor establish this.

Understand the demographics of the curriculum's intended audience.  There are a number of factors that will affect how the curriculum is received. Age, gender and religion all play a part, as do the student's racial, ethical and cultural backgrounds.

In the curriculum design setting, age can be an especially important consideration. Younger audiences demand constant interaction and a "wow" factor that has been nurtured by the Internet and video games.   They also respond well to learning that takes a competitive approach.

Don't be afraid to develop multiple versions of presentations or student materials that can be applied to specific audiences. Keep student learning outcomes and information consistent, but students will appreciate the effort to present information in a manner consistent with their need.

Even more important than a demographic understanding of the audience, good curriculum design must take into consideration the situation the audience will be in for the activity.  Will the material be delivered online?  In a classroom to 24 students?  In an outside open area, from a stage, to 100 people? Each of these training scenarios requires tweaks to how the information is presented and should be addressed in the curriculum.   Instructors appreciate when a curriculum design takes into account potential pitfalls, and gives them ideas and tools for adapting to situational changes.

Instructors may not always be able to control some situational aspects, such as timing of an activity. Every instructor has had to follow a truly outstanding presenter, or teach immediately after the dreaded lunch break. Good curricula provide tips and tricks to help overcome these situations. Be sure any selected or developed program gives training center staff the flexibility to adapt without compromising the student learning outcomes.

The last thing a training manager should keep in mind when developing or evaluating curricula is the audience's disposition toward the topic. Are they interested? What is their attitude about being part of the training and the topic? What is their existing knowledge level? One of the most common mistakes in curriculum design is trying to create material that is too universal – the experienced students get very disheartened when training consists of the lowest level information and doesn't challenge them. Likewise, tailoring a curriculum only to experienced providers may mean the one new person in the room feels alienated.

## Provide Good Information

No amount of planning, whiz-bang graphics, or interactivity can make up for inconsistent, incomplete, or inaccurate information. Information should also be timely. Students tend to be savvy consumers, picking up on even tiny details such as dated photographs.

---

**Incomplete, Inconsistent, or Inaccurate = Ineffective**

---

Be sure the information is from credible sources. As helpful as the *Wikipedia* web site is, posted information is not always accurate or current. Even global news leaders such as CNN and NBC have been fooled by seemingly factual information that turned out to be incorrect. Always verify information with the original source or document. Be sure to keep a record of, and give proper credit to, sources of information.

The development group can be especially useful in helping identify potentially questionable information or positions. When the group provides information or comments, take one of three courses of action:

1. Agree with the comment or change after doing research and documenting the reasons for agreement with it; documentation of the change and rationale are especially important if the change affects a critical step, common belief or strongly polarizing viewpoint.
2. Reject the comment or suggestion. Be sure reasons and resources are cited to back up the rejection.
3. Make a change to the curriculum based on the comment, but not necessarily the change that was suggested.

A Microsoft Excel spreadsheet can be an excellent tool to track changes during the development process. Include columns in which to paraphrase the comment or change, the source of the comment, the dates the comment was received and addressed, what changes (if any) were made, and source of supporting information. Creating this type of documentation in support of the finished project will help ensure credibility if training materials are ever challenged.

When using photographs or videos, many developers lose sight of the fact the training materials are trying to teach an audience the proper behavior. They include "funny" photos or videos of things that happen when students fail to apply the knowledge, skills or abilities being taught. Showing a $300,000 truck submerged in a pond definitely illustrates what can happen when the driver doesn't perform – but does it teach future drivers how to avoid the situation? Remember to design materials so that the student is exposed to positive behaviors the instructor wants them to emulate.

---

**Good content shows good behavior.**

---

Many developers have gotten into the habit of including multiple video clips in their materials. First, be sure to have appropriate legal permission for use or display of the clip. Simply because the originator of the content posted it to YouTube™ does not make the clip public domain or permit use it in training materials. Even simply linking directly to the site can create permissions issues. If using video to teach a specific skill, use a staged video first, clearly breaking the task down into specific steps. Follow that with a video of the skill being used in real life. Be sure any clips are narrated. Many instructors tend to talk right through video in a classroom setting and frequently miss key points the developer intended – no matter how good the curricula's lecture notes are constructed. Remember that clips set in real life often contain skill performance errors; acknowledge those mistakes but keep the focus on the steps that are done correctly.

### Curricula and Copyrights
Instructional designers and content developers have a wealth of resources today, thanks to the internet. Copyright law hasn't changed, though. The creator of an original work of authorship is granted a set of exclusive legal rights, whether the author is an individual or a company. Copyright law is notoriously complex, but there are three focal points that every training center needs to be aware of. For further research, consult the U.S. Copyright Office or an intellectual property specialist.

### Content from the Internet
Illustrations, photographs, and videos abound on the World Wide Web. Many of today's training sessions contain internet-based content. Just because something is found on the internet does not make the content public domain. Common ideas, documented facts, words, and government work such as judicial opinions or administrative rulings are generally public domain; so are most works created by federal government employees as part of their official responsibility.

**Being available on the Internet doesn't make content public domain.**

A lot of the content available on the web is posted without the knowledge or permission of the actual copyright owner.  Training centers may have a very difficult time differentiating between legally obtained and infringing material.

Some tips:

1.   Obtain content directly from the creator through a legitimate site.
2.   Attribute the content to the creator or copyright holder.
3.   Use great care when using public file-sharing sites such as YouTube; just because someone posts the content doesn't mean they are the legal copyright holder.
4.   Quality content is rarely free; especially for commercial use.
5.   Review end-user license agreements, even for photos purchased from a stock agency or "free" clip art.  In many cases the license is restrictive, especially for commercial use.

There has been a lot of emphasis on *Fair Use* by educators in the classroom.  Use for nonprofit educational purposes is only one element of the fair use test. Many instructors and staff members may take the attitude "nobody really cares." They do.  A small, for profit computer training firm in Michigan was successfully sued under copyright law; the case revolved around the training center's use of software and trademarks as part of its business activity. (Dassault Systems, SA v. Childress, 2011).  There are numerous examples of case law associated with the principles of fair use. (Stanford University, 2012).

Copyright law is fairly explicit in both what rights are reserved to the author and what constitutes a permitted fair use. Training centers must be aware of the information being presented both in the classroom and through any web or learning portals.

*Avoiding Copyright Issues*
So what's the best way to avoid copyright issues?

Create Your Own Content
The easiest way to avoid copyright issues is to create the content.  Creating photographs, graphics, and video or animation ensures the training center has clear ownership.  Although content creation requires time, effort and expense the content tends to be of greater educational value.

Get Permission or Clearance
When it comes to copyright law,  one of the best ways to ensure the legality of content is to obtain permission from the copyright owner. This process is referred to as "clearing the rights".  Obtaining clearance to use a photograph or article is relatively easy, but not usually free.  For publications such as periodicals or books, visit the Copyright Clearance

Center.  For music, contact the publisher (label) of the song.  For video clips, start with the production company that created the content.  Most major publishers and production companies deal with rights and clearance requests frequently and appreciate those who reach out and respect the value of copyrighted material.  Be specific in how the copyrighted material will be used. Obtaining permission to play a song during a convention session is very different from synchronizing an artist's performance to photographs and video taken by students or training center staff members.

Protect Your Own Content

Training centers rarely think about protecting the work developed as part of the training process.  Training curricula and materials are valuable.  Under the law, once a work is created and fixed in a tangible form, it is protected. Although registration is not required in order for the content to be protected, registration is recommended. Registration ensures that the basic data surrounding the work is part of the public record. Registration also permits the content to serve as *prima facie* evidence should the need to enforce a copyright ever arise.

One of the more difficult areas for a training center to navigate is ownership of content. Whether it comes from a development team working on the latest online courses, or from an independently contracted instructor who developed a great classroom presentation - the training center must know who actually "owns" the content.  This should be clearly established by written agreements.

> *Case Study:  A Case of Mixed Up Rights*
>
> An independently contracted instructor takes a photograph of two workers performing a maintenance operation at a client's work site.  The client's logo is visible on both the equipment and worker's clothing. The photograph is subsequently inserted into a training presentation.  The training center's advertising department likes the photograph, and subsequently uses it marketing materials.  If rights aren't clearly defined, this situation can cost the center a client, an instructor, and many hours on the phone. First, anyone taking photos or video for inclusion in a training program should attain a model release from everyone visible in the photograph.  If the training center or instructor doesn't own the location, obtain a location release from the property owner.  If a logo or brand is visible in the photo, there are two choices:  obtain permission (license) from the owner(s), or edit the photograph.  Finally, the agreement with the instructor should clearly define who owns the photograph once it is inserted into the training program and delivered at the training center.

In many cases, employees specifically tasked by the training center with creating content are not considered the factual author. The content can be considered the employee's work product; the training center itself is then considered the author.  When working with independently contracted professionals, remember that the training center is the client and generally has the expectation to fully own the content. If developing content, have an attorney specializing in intellectual property review or create documents specifically to protect the training center's ownership of content. Have an honest discussion with staff and instructors when they join the training organization, so they understand organizational policy on intellectual property.

Some additional resources on intellectual property and copyright can be found at:

- The Copyright Clearance Center
  http://www.copyright.com
- Stanford University
  http://fairuse.stanford.edu
- University of Maryland University College Library
  http://www.umuc.edu/library/libhow/copyright.cfm
- US Copyright Office
  http://www.copyright.gov

The audio and video elements of training programs can be timely and costly, but the impact of those elements is significant. Especially with younger audiences, taking the time to develop and include good A/V elements can help engage the audience and increase the transfer of information.

## Remembering vs. Forgetting

A lot of instructional designers and instructors are brought up believing that people remember 20 percent of what they see, 30 percent of what they hear, and 80 percent of what they do. This belief is totally incorrect. The examples of this misrepresentation are alarming, and even propagate through educational institutions. The percentages are a myth. (Thalheimer, People remember 10%, 20%...Oh Really?, 2006).

Wasn't it odd that charts supporting this theory almost always show 10% increments? There is very little chance that any legitimate research would produce such an exact breakdown. Research Edgar Dale's *Cone of Experience*, often cited as the basis of "percentage" standard. Dale's original model was subjective. Dale warned against taking the model too literally. (Dale, 1969). So what were Dale's points? First, good curriculum design involves a variety of teaching methods so that all students have an opportunity to learn. Second, each element of a curriculum should build off previous elements.

**There is no current research to support claims that any one method of instruction is superior to another.**

Hermann Ebbinghaus' *Memory: A Contribution to Experimental Psychology* brings up an additional point. A key factor in training isn't getting students to remember what is taught – the goal is to prevent the student from forgetting.

Keeping good students from forgetting good information is not as challenging as one might think. Keep the content highly personal. Just because a student is learning via distributed technology does not mean the material has to be cold and impersonal. Good curriculum design dictates that the message is delivered in a manner that makes a strong impact on the audience. Simply put, always build a link between the students and subject. Deliver good information using good instructional techniques.

## Use Pilot Programs

The process of obtaining feedback on a program while still under development is known as *formative evaluation*. Once the draft curriculum is in hand, work with a small group of individuals to validate the program before its' final release. If the goal is to deliver a quality program, use a small group of students to get a formative evaluation. These are also often referred to as "pilot programs." These programs are most effective if the student has opportunity to put the training into practice immediately following the session. Remember that training centers are not restricted to a single pilot program – if the first program comes back with substantial changes, it is perfectly acceptable to rework the project and run an additional pilot.

Maintain close contact with students participating in any formative evaluation program, especially if the course is lengthy. Share the feedback from the pilot students with the peer development group.

So what kind of questions might be asked in a pilot program?

- Did the graphics, video, music, narration, etc. support the student learning outcomes, or confuse you?
- Did you understand what the program wanted you to be able to do, or do better – after training?
- Did the program succeed in helping you gain a new skill or ability?
- Were there any inconsistencies or inaccuracies in the program?
- Did the program reflect the way this will happen in real life?

## Overcoming Managers and Supervisors

Another hurdle the training manager has to overcome is the manager or supervisor that draws a distinction between the "business side" and training. These individuals are a critical link in a worker's ability to put information from training into practice on the job.

A training manager has four tools to help overcome this viewpoint, and improve transfer of training. These actions also build a stronger relationship between training programs and the work environment.

### Participating in Training

How should managers and supervisors participate in training? Each organization or type of business is different, but there are ways to involve these individuals in training.

*Participation in Program Development*

The individuals responsible for selecting or developing training curricula should routinely involve managers and supervisors. Managers are frequently a strong contributor to peer review groups, especially when there is a need to create realistic scenarios. Don't limit participation to reviewing documents. Keeping managers engaged throughout the process builds feelings of ownership of the process and material. Involvement in the development process can also prepare them to assist in teaching the content initially and monitoring skill performance on a daily basis.

*Utilization as Instructors*

Many instructors agree that in a workplace class, students who have extensive experience or authority can be a significant distraction during training. Managers and supervisors often have gross misconceptions about training, such as "anybody can be a trainer" or "the training department is a place to put poor performers". (Mager, 1996).

Combat this misconception by changing their role in the classroom from student to instructor. Integrate these individuals into the training program as skill instructors or other assistant roles. Provide a basic training or coaching workshop for managers and supervisors. When teaching a workplace skill, a manager or supervisor can provide great insight to students.

### Monitoring Workplace Skill

Measuring how well a student transfers training from the classroom to the job can be difficult. Trainers pass through worksites or areas infrequently and rarely have the time necessary to observe employees on the job. Supervisor and managers operate in this environment daily. Part of a supervisor or manager's responsibility should be workplace skill monitoring. Things to look for:

- A decrease in productivity
- A decrease in the quality of the work being performed
- Changes in work habits, such as safety violations or attendance problems

Any of these indicators can be identified by a well-trained manager or supervisor. Not all monitoring has to be for negative behaviors or change. Supervisor should be equally aware for positive changes. An employee with a sudden increase in production without a change in work quality may have found a process improvement. Supervisors and managers are instrumental in passing those ideas back to the training center for inclusion in future programs.

### Documenting Performance

Another element that frustrates managers and supervisors is paperwork. Training managers want feedback on how an employee performs at work. Feedback is typically associated with documentation. Documentation often means paper, computer, or internet-based forms that require the supervisor to sit in an office.

These methods of documenting performance are impractical, even for the training manager. Feedback is rarely accurate or timely. Taking supervisors or managers away from the work area mean being away from their primary responsibility; production, safety, and quality can all be affected.

When it comes to compliance with regulations on programs like hearing conservation or forklift operation, performance documentation is extremely important. A supervisor observing and documenting the employee working safely at a specific point in time demonstrates more than training - it demonstrates a culture of safety.

Mobile technologies such as the smart phone and tablet computer are changing the way performance is documented. Allowing managers and supervisors to document workplace skills without taking them out of the work environment is a growing trend. Documenting performance into a learning management system using mobile technology is less threatening to workers than formal evaluations or formal remediation.

Timely documentation of employee performance from supervisors and managers allows training managers to make informed decisions about training. Capturing timely data allows for a detailed workplace skills analysis. A supervisor's documentation can uncover trends important to training that might otherwise be missed.

### Providing Remediation and Coaching

Training manages can further involve supervisors by encouraging them to provide remediation and coaching on the job. Supervisors and managers are equal parts motivator, teacher, and evaluator. When problems are identified, remediation can be provided on the spot as long as the managers and supervisors are fully invested in the training center's programs. Teach students formally then give managers latitude to reinforce training on the job.

---

**Providing employees constructive feedback that corresponds directly to training programs is a manager or supervisor responsibility.**

---

Training managers benefit from having managers and supervisors engaged as part of the training center. They become a primary source of feedback for the training center, and can be training's strongest advocate.

## Evaluate & Update

Evaluation is a basic function of instructional design, and takes many forms.

- The competency of each student is evaluated relative to student learning outcomes, both during training and on the job.
- Instructor development must be guided by an ongoing assessment of instructors as both individuals and as a group.

- Courses and curricula are assessed for correlation with job expectations and return on investment.
- The effectiveness of the training center as a whole must be evaluated against corporate strategy and goals.

### Student Evaluation

Measuring student performance against the curriculum's desired outcome(s) is usually a function of the instructor staff. The curriculum will typically specify how the student will be evaluated.

Training managers should routinely observe student evaluation processes and understand how students perform. Specific data points the training manager should monitor:

- How did the students in a class perform, compared to each other?
- How did students in a class perform compared to students in a different class on the same subject? If there are statistically significant differences, why?
- How do all students in all classes compare to the curriculum's desired outcome?
- Look for patterns in students, instructors and classes.

### Transfer of Training

Transfer of training refers to how the students apply the information from a training program once they return to the work environment. Training center staff should routinely observe students in the work environment. Transfer of training is a key metric for training centers.

Look for barriers that prevent a student from transferring training to the job. Common barriers to transfer include working conditions, a lack of peer support, or a lack of management support.

#### Working Conditions

Working conditions become a barrier to transfer when:

- Training doesn't actually mirror the job expectations
- Tools, equipment, or machinery are inadequate or differ from training
- Time or quality pressures are introduced
- The job involves exposure to weather (heat, cold, rain, etc.)
- The student has few opportunities to use skills

Mismatches between the work environment and training often occur when the training center relies on antiquated or broken equipment salvaged as training props. Invest in realistic training props.

## Lack of Peer Support

When a student returns to the workplace, peers can quickly affect a student's application of new knowledge or skills. Transfer is difficult when a student's peers view training as a waste of time; fail to provide feedback; or discourage use on the job.

A classic example involves the use of safety equipment; a student is taught the proper policy and use of a fall arrest device in training. The student is subsequently ridiculed by coworkers for using the device on the actual job.

## Lack of Management Support

A lack of management support also quickly erodes a student's application of training to the job. Supervisors may be apathetic or unsupportive of training. Managers may not accept a student's new knowledge or skills, or allow them to apply the information to the job.

Even more detrimental to transfer are supervisors or managers that fail to provide meaningful feedback on the job. Manager feedback that is inconsistent with the training program is a common problem.

## Overcoming Barriers

Many of the barriers are relationship or behavioral issues that are not changed overnight. The best place to overcome the barriers is in the classroom as the knowledge and skills are presented.

---

**Be sure the curriculum addresses known barriers in the classroom and evaluation.**

---

When students are evaluated incorporate scenarios that mimick the known barriers. Explain how to approach situations where they are blocked from applying their training. Provide students with techniques to overcome the issues.

## Instructor Evaluation

Evaluating instructors often falls to the bottom of the training manager's to-do list. Training managers are frequently in the classroom yet rarely provide quality feedback to the instructional staff.

There are a number of options to help training managers provide feedback to the instructor staff.

### Student Evaluations

Student evaluations of instructor performance are often in an end-of-course evaluation tool. The tool should be designed so that there is a clear distinction between feedback on the course as a whole and individual instructor performance. If a course is taught by multiple instructors, training managers may have a hard time distinguishing which instructor was being addressed. Student evaluations can be highly subjective, but can also provide insights into issues that may not be identified by any other methods.

*Staff Evaluations*

Staff evaluations are the most formal of the instructor evaluation tools. These tools are completed by training center staff members who directly observe instructor performance. Often, feedback is provided to the instructor immediately after being observed. On the down side, staff members may only observe for one or two out of multiple class meeting periods.

Instructors are often aware that the evaluation is being done, so instructor behavior may be different than in an unobserved session. The number of staff members qualified to conduct instructor evaluations can limit the effectiveness of the process; i.e., even active instructors might only get evaluated annually. Negative staff evaluations can also be viewed as punitive rather than constructive.

*Peer Evaluations*

Peer evaluations are becoming more commonplace. In the academic arena, faculty members on track for tenure are routinely observed by peers and provided both formal and informal feedback. Instructors may find peer evaluations less intrusive and less threatening than staff evaluations. Some training managers are requiring instructors to conduct peer evaluations as part of the criteria to maintain their own instructor status.

*Self-Evaluations*

Instructor self-evaluations have also become popular. Instructors are provided a tool that they complete and submit to the training center after conducting a training session. Self-evaluation tools often ask the instructor to identify weaknesses and state a plan for improvement.

*Setting up an Evaluation System*

Instructors need to receive specific, timely feedback on performance. Training centers often use a combination of these evaluation methods to gather information on instructors. Information gained from the evaluation process can be used to create both individual and center-wide instructor development plans.

*Curricular Evaluation*

Training managers should be collecting feedback about each ongoing course or curriculum. Developing or acquiring a program is a significant expense, and every training organization wants to maximize the return on its investment. Careful evaluation early during implementation eye minimizes the impact of errors or omissions.

---

**Curricula should be evaluated after delivery of the first programs and on a defined schedule (normally every two to three years) after that.**

---

Changes to a program should be made on a scheduled basis, unless a critical change occurs outside of the normal review process. Changes of a critical nature are triggered by significant events, such as a new machine or identification of a life safety issue. The curriculum developer should know what events merit a change immediately, versus a change in the next update cycle.

Keep a list of suggestions and changes in a spreadsheet so that when the development group is ready to update the program, they have a solid starting point.

Many instructional designers and curriculum planners update content too frequently. Consider the student's perspective. Most programs are not that dynamic – frequently changing material can be perceived by students that the original program wasn't well thought out.

### The Course and Work Performance

Will Thalheimer says "Despite decades of advocacy by our best trade associations, our wisest gurus, and our most practical researchers, most organizations today still rely on training courses that have little impact in promoting on-the-job performance."

Training managers are ultimately charged with leading training organizations that have a positive effect on the corporate entity. Planning a curriculum, getting the right students to class, and ensuring training transfers to the job are all tasks that should lead towards improvements for the corporate entity as a whole.

Evaluating a course consists of more than collecting student feedback at the end of each class session. The evaluation form in Figures 1 and 2, downloadable from Thalheimer's web site, outlines a thorough course evaluation process focusing on five areas:

- Course Content
- Course Outcomes
- Evaluation Methods
- Course Design
- Course Integration

### Updating the Curriculum

Feedback from throughout the evaluation process should be provided to the peer group. How students and instructors performed both in training and on the job must be what drives the curriculum update.

## Course Review Template—Does Your Course Boost Work Performance?

© Copyright 2011 by Will Thalheimer
Phone: 888-579-9814
Email: info@work-learning.com

Work-Learning Research, Inc.
www.work-learning.com
www.willatworklearning.com

| Research-Inspired Practices | Rationale | Self-Rating | Provide Proof |
|---|---|---|---|
| **Is the Content Right?** | **Why Important?** | **Circle the Truth** | **Specify How Achieved** |
| Is there a <u>clearly recognized need</u> indicating this content will <u>support actual on-the-job performance</u>? | We should teach with a performance purpose. | YES   NO<br>*Points=2* | |
| Has the <u>content been verified</u> as relevant by professionals working in the field <u>within the last year</u>? | Content must be up-to-date. | YES   NO<br>*Points=1* | |
| Has the content been <u>cross checked</u> with other courses and been found to be <u>non-redundant</u>? | Reinforcement is okay, but redundancy is costly. | YES   NO<br>*Points=1* | |
| **Are there Clear Performance-Related Goals?** | **Why?** | **Circle the Truth** | **Specify How Achieved** |
| Is this course intended to <u>meet compliance requirements</u>, provide <u>general awareness</u> or improve <u>on-the-job performance?</u> | It is better to have a higher percentage of courses that support actual on-the-job performance. | Compliance (0)<br>Awareness (1)<br>Performance (3)<br>*Points in ( ) above* | |
| Does the course have a clear <u>on-the-job performance outcome</u> specified? | We ought to know what we're aiming to accomplish. | YES   NO<br>*Points=2* | |
| **Is Measurement Effective in Enabling Course Improvement?** | **Why?** | **Circle the Truth** | **Specify How Achieved** |
| Has an overarching <u>evaluation objective</u> been identified to guide course evaluation? | A general objective can guide meaningful evaluation. | YES   NO<br>*Points=3* | |
| Are <u>end-of-course learner responses</u> gathered to measure satisfaction and sense of value/relevance? | Smile sheets are valuable in measuring learner satisfaction. | YES   NO<br>*Points=1* | |
| Are <u>after-course on-the-job learner responses</u> gathered to measure the learners' assessment of their success in applying the learning to their job? | These delayed smile sheets can get the learners' sense of how application is going, also noting obstacles & success factors. | YES   NO<br>*Points=2* | |
| Do we have evaluation methods that tell us <u>whether learners remember</u> what they've learned after a week or more from the end of training? | Application of learning requires that the learners remember what they learned. | YES   NO<br>*Points=3* | |
| Does the course require learners to produce <u>real work products to some criterion of success</u>? | Real on-the-job work products, judged for success, show relevance to performance. | YES   NO<br>*Points=2* | |
| Does the course track whether <u>actual on-the-job performance</u> improved on the targeted skills? | The gold standard. Subjective opinions don't count much! | YES   NO<br>*Points=3* | |
| **Is the Course Well Designed?** | **Why?** | **Circle the Truth** | **Specify How Achieved** |
| Does the course engage the learners in a way that <u>maximizes attention</u> on important concepts/skills? | Focused attention is necessary for learning. | YES   NO<br>*Points=1* | |
| Do the <u>course facilitators</u> (if any) <u>exude credibility</u>, being both competent and trustworthy? Do the <u>course materials exude credibility</u>, having good production values, being organized, having trustworthy content? | Credibility is critical to enable sustained attention and motivation within the learning process. | YES   NO<br>*Points=2* | |
| Does the course require learners to <u>demonstrate their understanding</u> by giving them significant practice with <u>realistic scenarios, simulations, or real-world situations</u>—and then <u>providing meaningful feedback</u>? | Since understanding is a key goal for training, when learners show that understanding, we validate success and provide feedback to learners. | YES   NO<br>*Points=3* | |
| Does the course support <u>long-term remembering</u> by providing <u>delayed realistic practice</u> and <u>repetitions spaced over time</u>? | Remembering is a key goal, so courses should be designed to support long-term remembering. | YES   NO<br>*Points=2* | |
| Does the course <u>motivate on-the-job performance</u> of the targeted skills? | Learners have to be more than skilled. They have to be willing & eager to apply their learning. | YES   NO<br>*Points=1* | |
| Does the course provide <u>prompting mechanisms</u> (like job aids) and have the learners practice using those job aids in realistic exercises in the course? | Repeated retrieval practice bolsters remembering. | YES   NO<br>*Points=2* | |

**1:  Course Review Template**
**(Thalheimer, Is Your Training Course Likely to Boost Performance?, 2011)**

| Integration with the Workplace | Why? | Circle the Truth | Specify How Achieved |
|---|---|---|---|
| Have the course instructors spent at least 80 hours within the last year embedded in workplace situations targeted by the course content? | To ensure that course content is relevant and instructors can act as workplace advocates, they should spend time in the field observing the reality. | YES   NO<br>Points=1 | |
| Do the learners' supervisors know the course content sufficiently to support and encourage the learners to properly apply the learning to the job? | Learners are more likely to apply what they've learned if they have their supervisors support and encouragement. | YES   NO<br>Points=1 | |
| Are learners' supervisors prompted to encourage and monitor the learners' efforts in applying the learning, both before the course and after? | Learners are more likely to apply what they've learned if they have their supervisors support and encouragement. | YES   NO<br>Points=2 | |
| After the bulk of the formal learning experience, are learners periodically reminded of course content and importance of utilizing or revisiting what they learned? | Learners are more likely to remember & apply what they've learned if they are periodically reminded on the job. | YES   NO<br>Points=2 | |
| Are there reference materials (or other courses) available to and used by learners after the course to enable them to deepen and reinforce their learning? | Learners often need multiple encounters with a topic to truly understand at a deep level. | YES   NO<br>Points=1 | |
| Are learners utilizing prompting mechanisms (either course-generated or self-generated) to ensure performance on the job? | Prompting mechanisms are effective to the extent that they are effectively utilized. | YES   NO<br>Points=2 | |
| Do learners have and utilize coaches within their workspace to help them in applying the learning? Are these coaches skilled in providing such guidance? | For most skills that are learned, it helps to have someone to provide guidance, feedback, and support while applying the learning to the actual work. | YES   NO<br>Points=2 | |
| Are learners measured objectively in using their new skills? Are they getting useful feedback of their actual job performance? | Learners will develop their skills more effectively on the job if they get good feedback. | YES   NO<br>Points=2 | |
| Do the course facilitators (or developers if no facilitators) keep in touch with the learners to determine their successes, and learn what obstacles they are facing as they apply the learning? | Keeping in touch with learners enables facilitators to respond to learning outcomes—by either directly intervening or by making course improvements. | YES   NO<br>Points=3 | |
| **How Does Your Course Measure Up?** | | | |
| Count up all the points your course earned. Feel free to give an item partial credit to better exemplify the result you feel it deserves.<br>Remember, these numbers aren't precise indicators. They are provided to give you a general idea of how you're doing. Don't get hung up on the numeric outcome. We recommend that you set a target and work to achieve improvement. | | Total Points Possible<br><br>50 | Points Earned?<br><br>_____ |
| | Rank 1 – Performance Demoting | 0-12 | Circle The Rank Earned by Your Course |
| | Rank 2 – Performance Stagnating | 13-20 | |
| | Rank 3 – Performance Nudging | 21-26 | |
| | Rank 4 – Performance Promoting | 27-32 | Post Your Results at:<br>http://tinyurl.com/CR-Template |
| | Rank 5 – Performance Boosting | 33-40 | |
| | Rank 6 – Performance Accelerating | 41-50 | |
| What is your conclusion? What is your next step? | | | |

Use this job aid to understand, benchmark, and improve your current practices. Send feedback to Dr. Will Thalheimer info@work-learning.com

**2: Course Review Template**
**(Thalheimer, Is Your Training Course Likely to Boost Performance?, 2011)**

# THE RIGHT TECHNOLOGY

"Technology is very seductive, and it is certainly changing the way things are designed and made and taught. The problem is when technology has seduced you away from thinking about things as deeply as you should." – Arthur Ganson

Two things enter a trainer's mind when technology is mentioned: Microsoft PowerPoint™ and an LCD projector. These are only two of the technological tools that training managers have to be concerned with. Proper application of technology to education and training can be a powerful, positive influence on the student's experience.

Proper application of technology brings four distinct benefits to a training program:

## Engage
Technology allows the training staff to engage students in a manner that appeals to them. In today's world, high-speed internet, complex mobile devices, and easy access to information are almost universally available. Training professionals need to leverage technology to engage the learner frequently using familiar technology. A variety of inexpensive tools allow today's curriculum developers to create dynamic, engaging course materials.

## Expand
Technology expands the walls of the classroom exponentially. Students have access to information, instantly, on their mobile devices. Communication tools such as broadcast e-mails, text messaging, and discussion threads expand the ability of students to interact and discuss topics outside of the class' schedule. Students are no longer restricted by geography or even language – remote attendance via the web has largely replaced video-based courses and tele-classes.

## Encourage
The accessibility and ease of use associated with today's technology encourages interaction between students, the training organization, and instructors.

## Evaluate
Technology allows training organizations to evaluate each student's attainment of outcome more effectively than ever. Complex branching scenarios, including video and audio, can easily be used. Adaptive testing, once restricted to the purest of academic environments, is now widespread. Advanced situation-based simulators are commonly found in health care, law enforcement, and manufacturing.

There are six key areas where technology impacts training and the training manager:

- Management & Development
- Presentation Software
- Technology In the Classroom
- Data Management
- Distributed Learning

## Management & Development

Technology has dramatically changed the curriculum development process. Today's training manager and curriculum developers need a number of technology-based tools.

### Computer Hardware

A little extra budget will pay dividends over time. Even though a low-end workstation may run all the necessary software, the time spent waiting for video or an executable file to render will quickly justify the added expense for a higher-end computer. Contrary to popular belief, both Microsoft Windows and Apple Mac platforms perform very well, when paired with the right software.

- A computer with a reasonably fast processor, large hard drive, lots of RAM, and an above-average video card.
- Two large monitor displays (20" or larger). During development, use one monitor to display the actual content creation software, the second for reference material (the web, lecture notes, etc.).
- An external hard drive dedicated to backing up the primary development computer, and serving as an archive for older items. Also consider an online backup service – a remotely accessible archive allows the retrieval of critical files if needed. For example, an online service is critical in the event a trainer's laptop is stolen while traveling.
- An backup power supply, to allow the safe shutdown of systems without losing content.
- A higher-quality set of headphones, for listening to and editing audio, and a quality microphone. Avoid combination headsets. Again, a small investment in the quality of the recording equipment will improve audio quality and clarity.
- If working with photographs or graphic design, consider acquiring and learning to use a graphics tablet in addition to a mouse.

### Software

A training manager needs a robust software library, even if not directly involved in the instructional design process. Although each training professional will develop preferences, being familiar with a wide variety of products can be extremely useful. Training managers benefit from having the same tools used by the instructional design team, especially if work is being outsourced or done on a billable basis. The ability to correct a simple mistake quickly and easily, without having to rely on external or non-departmental personnel saves time and budget.  Some basic software needs include:

- Microsoft Office, including Word, Excel, and PowerPoint as a minimum.
- Content creation software. If software or online demonstrations are a frequent task, consider packages that record the computer screen and mouse movements automatically.
- Video capture, editing, and conversion software. Invest in quality programs, especially if converting video from one format to another. Although there are free tools available, investing a small amount will yield better quality video and smaller file sizes.
- Audio editing software.
- All common Internet browsing platforms – Internet Explorer, Firefox, Chrome, Opera, and Safari.

## Collaboration Tools

Collaboration with peers and stakeholders is a core element for many training managers. Web-based meeting services such as GoToMeeting, Connect Pro, or WebEx are very useful beyond delivery of training. Web meeting services allow for feedback from a variety of users, even on short notice. Be aware of the limitations of web meeting services. Some services have trouble handling video unless it's converted to a specific format; others may only be able to import specific document types.

There are a variety of both free and low-cost services that allow collaboration. Often these come with file size limitations, or limits on the number of collaborators.  In these cases, training managers are often limited to working within a particular developer's suite – such as Microsoft's Office™ applications or Adobe's Acrobat family.

Many software packages used to develop class materials have built-in tools to facilitate reviews and comments. For example, a Microsoft PowerPoint™ presentation can be emailed to multiple recipients, and revisions or comments merged into a single document for review.

Most curriculum developers that work with online course delivery are familiar with the sharable content object reference model (SCORM).  Most development packages will publish SCORM-conformant content that can be easily uploaded into training / learning management systems.  Many of these same development software packages are closely aligned with a specific training / learning management system. Publishing or playing content developed with something other than the developer's own training / learning management system can be frustrating if a project has been developed with a feature or tool that is proprietary to a single company.

# Presentation Software

Microsoft's PowerPoint™ and other tools that create presentations are powerful.  In the past, publishers and instructors had to put significant effort into creating visuals for a presentation.  Presentations were delivered using 35mm slide projectors or acetate overheads.  Educators were forced to deliver a reasonably consistent message because the costs and time associated with production were significant.   Presentation software and the Internet changed the time and cost components significantly.  Look around the next conference or symposium lobby and a presenter or two will likely be sitting in the atrium putting the "finishing touches" on a presentation.  The constant tweaking of a presentation right up to the point of delivery has a negative impact on the quality.

If using PowerPoint™ or other tool, the presentation should be completed at least 30 days before delivery.  Resist the urge to continue changing the message, focusing instead on practicing the delivery.

Educators who develop their own presentations should ensure the accuracy and timeliness of the information used in each presentation.  Although there are many legitimate resources, there is an equal amount of inaccurate or erroneous information. Be diligent in fact-checking and keep reference and source information. Do not rely on third-party sites that quote research – go to the source. Use care when paraphrasing information.  Training Managers have a responsibility to review instructor-developed presentations with a critical eye.

A simple online search returns many articles eschewing "rules" for visual presentations; these rules may govern font size, suggest font choices, recommend a number of slides, etc.  Simply put, these may be good resources but above all, the presentation must be visually appealing, professional appearing, and supporting of the speaker.  The PowerPoint itself is not the presentation; first and foremost, the slides are tools.  The presentation is what the instructor has to say – not what is projected on the screen.  The presentation slides were called *visual aids* in the past – the displayed information is there to reinforce and strengthen the message, not replace it. The individual presenter, not the laptop, is the educator.

The issues with computer-based presentations extend right up to the point of delivery. Many good messages have gone completely unnoticed because audio or video files didn't play properly, the room was too bright so the colors washed out, or because a computer and projector simply wouldn't work together.  Many of these issues are overcome through planning and preparation.

Developing a presentation for classroom delivery is just one part of curriculum development.  Today's training professionals have a wealth of tools available to them. From researching a potential topic to creating course materials and obtaining feedback, technology has affected the entire development process.

# Technology in the Classroom

Training managers typically are responsible for both obtaining and maintaining the technology found in the classroom. Today's instructors and students have complex demands in the classroom, based on the type of class being conducted.

## Integrated Technology

Some of today's classrooms have highly integrated systems. Although costly, these systems provide unparalleled flexibility for classroom space. These rooms typically have complex video and audio systems. Room controls can include temperature, lighting and even window shades. Video systems can include local television or satellite systems, DVD players, computers, or advanced video conferencing. Have someone familiar with the room and controls on hand to operate them.

---

**Remember, people rarely get in trouble for asking the owner of the equipment to operate or assist with complex or expensive audio-visual equipment.**

---

Be sure any video conferencing systems are placed in an inactive or disabled mode unless they are part of the class program. The sudden appearance of a corporate executive or inadvertent broadcast of a training session to a remote location can be a major distraction.

## Network and Internet Access

Virtually every classroom has internet access today, either through an Ethernet connection or Wi-Fi. For instructors, try to provide an Ethernet connection. This helps minimize bandwidth or connection issues for instructors utilizing external sites with video or media. Always recommend instructors test any links or sites prior to the start of a training session.

If the training center decides to allow instructors and/or students access to a wireless network, consider establishing separate networks for each. At a minimum, establish a network separate from the staff or primary training center. Students are quick to connect to public wireless networks with laptops, tablets, and mobile devices. By establishing separate networks, the instructor's bandwidth is unaffected by student network use.

Establish a network security policy for any instructor or student networks. Information Technology personnel should be able to assist in setting a simple security policy. At no time should non-employee students or instructors have access to the primary corporate network (unless they are an appropriately credentialed employee). Consider allowing instructor access to a single, centrally located printer or multi-function device.

Access to personal devices can also lead to distracted, inattentive students. Laptops, mobile phones, and tablets are excellent resources when used properly. Anticipate the technology students will bring to class, and plan for it.

Training managers should also consider investing in a wireless "hotspot". These small devices are available from most major wireless providers. The speed may be slightly slower than a traditional Internet connection, but provide secure and reliable backup Internet source. Corporate IT infrastructures are generally reliable but these devices provide an excellent backup plan. Hotspots can also be very useful when training must be conducted in non-traditional environments.

### SMART™ Boards

Interactive boards (SMART™ boards) have found their way into many academic and corporate classrooms. These boards double as a screen for displaying a presentation and whiteboard. Be sure instructors are familiar with the board's operation before being assigned to teach in a room where these boards are available. One common mistake unfamiliar instructors make is the use of incorrect markers - replacing a board's surface is expensive. As a training manager, it's a good idea to remove any markers that could potentially damage the board from the classroom.

Many interactive boards are connected to laptop or other computer. Instructors should transfer material to the computer rather than attempt connecting the board to their own laptop. Transferring materials from a CD, DVD, or USB drive to the host computer is often more reliable and effective. Another option is to place the instructor's material on a shared network location, accessible by the host computer.

As with other technologies, instructors should do a complete walk-through of presentation materials prior to the start of class. Training managers should accompany instructors in this walk-through, especially if the instructor is new. Invariably questions will arise, and being present will help prevent any frustrations.

### Video/Audio Recording

Today's smaller mobile devices and cameras capable of capturing hours of audio and video force educators  make it essential to develop a policy covering audio/video recordings. Instructors and training centers can easily record sessions for evaluation and e-learning. Students may also record sessions, potentially without the knowledge of the instructor or training center. Ensure that any policy is clearly communicated and deliver classes in a professional, ethical manner.

### Scenarios and Skills

Building skill and competency is easier than ever, as well. Technology has made simulation and reality-based training evolutions practical and affordable, especially in industries such as health care. The ability to develop complex, interactive branching scenarios is now available to most instructors. Whether delivered online or in a lab, complex scenarios and simulations allow students to develop problem-solving and critical thinking skills. If simulation tools or resources are cost-prohibitive, consider reaching out to others that could benefit from the same resource. Talk to academic institutions, or create a consortium to share in the costs.

Training environments are typically very dynamic. Instructional designers should always be clear about the technological resources necessary to deliver a program. If a presentation has a three-minute video narrated video clip, the curriculum should prompt instructors to have proper speakers or audio equipment.

Preparation is critical to avoiding issues. To overcome problems instructors and students can encounter, training managers need to be more prepared than the casual instructor. Keep these items handy:

- A surge-protected power strip
- 8" long cable (zip) ties
- AA, AAA, and 9V batteries (most professional wireless microphones use 9-volt batteries)
- Matte black 3" rigging tape (engineered to avoid peeling paint or leaving marks)
- A set of small powered speakers
- A USB mouse or presentation remote
- Minimum 6' Ethernet and USB printer cables
- 10' USB extension cable
- Video Cables: VGA, RCA (red, white, yellow) and HDMI cables
- Audio Cables: mini-to-RCA (red & white), mini-to-mini, RCA extension cable, and RCA female-to-male adapters.
  If teaching environments have built-in audio systems, consider adding appropriate patch cords
- Small slotted and Phillips-head screwdrivers
- A USB Thumb Drive (empty), minimum 8 GB size for helping instructors transfer files

## Data Management

Training data is valuable, and training centers generate volumes of it. Training managers rely on technology to manage the constant flow of information. The data helps the training manager market class offerings, sell books and materials, and ensure compliance. Data management tools tend focus on critical tasks of managing the training function, communicating with stakeholders, and delivering training offerings.

### Training / Learning Management Systems

There are a wide variety of systems in the marketplace today. Selecting the proper software is a critical decision. Generally, a system is employed to:

- Maintain records on students and classes taught
- Centralize and secure data
- Automate common tasks
- Allow delivery of online course or class offerings

- Administer exams and surveys

Good systems should manage the data on people, training activity, and resources. Systems should communicate information automatically to the appropriate parties. Information should be readily available through charts and reports. Solutions should allow delivery of content in support of classroom activity, or through self-paced classes. Appendix A, beginning on page 80, contains detailed information on learning management systems.

## Data Capture

Capturing training data can be a difficult challenge, especially for those organizations who conduct training "on the job" or in environments that make traditional, paper-based recordkeeping difficult. For example, an organization conducts multiple skill stations using multiple instructors. One option may be to give each student bar coded identification, and assigning the lead instructor for each station a bar-code reader. When a student demonstrates competency, the instructor scans the student's identification. Some systems capture information from an employee ID containing a bar code, radio-frequency identification (RFID), or magnetic stripe as a way of signing in and out of training, much like a time clock.

The use of mobile devices to capture student information is another paperless option. Whether logging on and simply entering attendance data during a class session or documenting skill proficiency on the job site, complex mobile devices such as phones and tablets can prove extremely useful to the training organization.

## Naming Conventions

Naming conventions are an often-overlooked aspect of data management. Trying to find a single file residing in a directory of 1000 others can be time consuming. Naming conventions are rarely a top priority for many training centers. Establishing rules governing course names and numbers, file names, and revisions can prove extremely beneficial. Using naming conventions, a computer's operating system can quickly find relevant files.

## Naming Conventions & a Learning Management System

So what areas of a learning management system benefit from consistent naming?

Common practices dictate that every staff member, instructor, and student be assigned a unique numerical identifier. The use of numbers that include elements of (or are even based upon) a social security number are highly discouraged. Some learning management systems use an Alternate ID field. A person's employee ID number may be used, but be cautious if the same number is used to access payroll or other sensitive information.

Create rules for using salutations and suffixes. Searching the database will be much easier if the formatting is consistent – for example, do users record a physician as "Dr.

John Smith" or "Janet Smith, M.D." If students self-enter their own profile information, delegate a staff member to review information on a daily or weekly basis.

Course numbering can provide a lot of information. Generally, U.S.-based colleges use a fairly consistent system. They use a four-character subject identifier, such as CJUS for Criminal Justice or ENGL for English. The subject identifier is followed by a course number. The first number indicates a relative difficult or level, 1 being the least difficult. Courses beginning with a 3 or 4 are usually upper-level courses. Courses starting with a 5 or higher would be graduate or doctorate level. The last number (the ones position) can be used contextually. Courses meant to be taken sequentially can be labeled that way, as in 201 and 202. Other systems may use the last number to represent a subset of the overall subject.

Item tags, tag clouds, and navigation categories are beneficial for students. A tag or category should match the subject, at a minimum. Think about how students will be searching for information.

Use naming conventions for locations and rooms. In many cases, this involves translating the information on a location to a shortened form for entry into the learning management system. Be consistent in how the shortened forms are created. When creating automated documents, be sure to include both location information and specific rooms.

Use file naming conventions for any supporting files uploaded to the learning management system.

## Naming Conventions & Content

One of the first steps to take is establishing a common storage area for files. Common areas can be set up easily on a network file server by the information technology department. Ensure training staff members have appropriate access for their role in the training center. For smaller centers, simply set up an external hard drive and share it among staff. The Digital Asset Management Learning Center provides an excellent best practices guide: http://www.damlearningcenter.com/best-practices-guide. Overall, naming conventions apply not only to individual files, but to folders also.

- Be sure there is an established procedure for backing up all data in at least one additional location.
- Establish a folder structure. Create a template outlining the desired structure and planning for the future. Start simply. Do not require 100 folders in a directory if 85 of them will be empty. Consider how individuals will be using the structure. Will a user be look for individual images or video clips more often than course creation files? A folder structure also improves performance during searches.

- Consider four main types of groupings: by subject, by process (course, class), by file type (audio, video, PDF), or role (developer, instructor).
- Do not allow people to "float" files to the top of the list using the special characters or numbers, such as the "_" character.
- Avoid redundancy. Do not store the same content in multiple places; good naming conventions and an established folder structure eliminate the need for duplication.

Consider using a temporary or working directory for active projects, or files that a large number of people will need frequent access to. If the training organization has a large development team, consider giving each person a "working" folder. Have the working folder synchronize with an appropriate area on the user's local hard drive. Differentiating working folders from the permanent library can be very useful; it also helps prevent a staff member from copying and using content that may still be under development.

Identify a member of the training center staff to act as a librarian for the center. The librarian monitors use of naming conventions, folder structures, synchronization, etc. The librarian can copy material from the working directories to the permanent library.

Those involved in production of documents should ALWAYS utilize version numbering. Software developers utilize a process where sections of software code must be "checked out" so that no other developer can work on that code. Some content development tools use a similar process. Ensure that staff members are clear on how to manage workflow. Current content should always be easily identifiable. Archive versions of key documents should be kept.

The actual file naming convention should be something universal throughout the training center. For example, audio or video assets could be named as "YearMonthDate_Subject_Type_Description.Ext". The subject is an abbreviated subject (potentially matching the naming convention for courses), while the type might be an abbreviation for type of footage (interview, b-roll, etc.). A second naming convention and folder structure might be used for actual class documents, such as presentations, documents, etc.

Generally, the file name should consist of the top two or three key elements that someone might be searching for. The most important element may is referred to as the anchor. Dates are often critical, both for identifying timely content and document retention purposes.

What's in a Name?
The most important part of a content naming convention is that all personnel in the center make use of it as an important tool for sharing of information and created content. Although fully integrated digital asset management is a growing trend, it can

be costly to implement. The basic principles can be easily applied using existing tools. Many of today's "gallery" tools allow for quick addition of descriptive tags and date information. These tools are helpful but are not a substitute for naming conventions. Gallery information is relative and software driven, while file naming conventions and folder locations represent a permanent solution.

## Distributed Learning Technology

Distributed learning through a variety of channels continues to gain acceptance. Research has shown that for many topics, well-developed online material is at least as effective as traditional face-to-face learning. (Noe, 2010) . Technologies available to training organizations include hybrid classes (where there is a mix of instructor-led and self-paced learning), instructor-led webinars, self-paced e-learning (interactive online classes), and self-paced classes based on videos, audio presentations, or documents.

Each of these technologies has value, depending on the training organization's business need. These types of training often involve extensive development or purchase from an external vendor. Some of the advantages of these types of technology include:

- Consistency:  The content is consistent for each student, and delivery of the content is consistent across all students.
- Accessibility:  The content is accessible from virtually any geographic location; elimination of most travel costs associated with delivery of training.
- Assessment & Feedback:  Depending on method used, there are increased opportunities to assess the individual student's knowledge and obtain feedback on class effectiveness

Potential disadvantages of distributed learning technologies include:

- Cost:  Programs can be expensive to develop or purchase initially; depending on technology can be expensive to update.
- Timeliness:  Can be difficult to update, depending upon technologies used.
- Learner Anxiety:  Not all learners are savvy in the use of technology; reliance on distributed learning places some learners at a significant disadvantage.

The training organization must take a hard look at the curriculum, the intended audience, and then apply technology that best suits the goal of the training program.

When using distributed learning technologies, consider a variety of factors that affect utilization.

### Technology Required

Be mindful of the technology required for the end user to access distributed learning programs.  Developers can create outstanding, highly interactive web classes – but if the student is using a dial-up connection and an older computer, he or she will get extremely frustrated waiting for content to load. Avoid using technology that requires the student to install software or special plug-ins.

## Collaboration Tools

No matter how inclusive or complete a distributed learning class seems to be, students will always have questions. Ensure that students know how to reach out to subject matter experts or instructors – and ensure those persons respond in an appropriate and timely manner.

## Return on Investment

Distributed learning programs can be expensive to develop and implement, the initial cost can seem daunting.  Training managers must be able to prove that training has a positive return on the corporate investment. Invest in technology or resources that can be used repeatedly throughout the organization. For example, don't invest in a lengthy, expensive video introduction for a single program; instead, consider a shorter video that can be used as a lead-in for multiple programs.

Avoid purchasing an expensive resource for a single purpose whenever possible; instead look for similar resources that can be repurposed or reused through a variety of training programs.

## Avoid Common E-Learning Mistakes

Developing quality e-learning content is not easy. There are some pitfalls in the distributed learning development process. Migrating from traditional instructor-led training creates real challenges for those tasked with creating an e-learning version. Here are five common distributed learning technology mistakes most of training managers have made.

### Mistake 1:  Using the Wrong Tools

Almost every e-learning development package includes a tool to rapidly import existing Microsoft PowerPoint presentations.  These tools should be labeled "For Emergency Use Only". Using the wrong tool to create a distributed learning class is just as dangerous as having poor content.

Instead, begin by deconstructing the existing materials.  Save images, video, and audio files for use in constructing the e-learning class. If starting without an existing presentation, begin by storyboarding or outlining the new class.

---

**No single tool performs every function an e-learning developer needs.**

---

The tools to create e-learning content vary widely in feature set and price.  Virtually every development tool offers a trial period, so take advantage of the trial and evaluate a number of products. Take a deconstructed presentation, and construct a distributed learning program.  Create the same program in a several different tools. Although time consuming, this exercise helps ensure proper selection of a good development platform that meets the organization's needs.

The same concept applies to identifying how the distributed learning class will be delivered. With an ever-growing number of services able to host content, try several before committing to a vendor. Some services do better with online video, others are more capable of handling international sessions. Some free services are available, such as *Join.Me*. Free services often come with file size limitations, limits on the number of participants, or carry advertisements.

Utilize small groups made up of instructors and students with recent experience in the class to help evaluate the tools.

### *Mistake 2: Poor Audio - Video Quality & Performance*
Audio and video are key elements of most distributed learning sessions. As such, they deserve as much attention as the presentation.

Audio is a source of frustration for many students. Volume changes between slides, unintelligible words, and background noise are all things within the developer's control. Some tips on audio:

1. Select a variety of individuals, both male and female, to be narrators for classes. Audition voices to the peer group. Select people that sound casual and relaxed, that speak clearly.
2. Use a quality microphone, positioned properly (normally 8-10" away).
3. Use a script. Print it out in a larger font (14-16 point) and leave plenty of white space.
4. Stand up while recording narration.
5. Use plenty of silence - before key passages and between takes. This makes it easier to edit clips.
6. Use closed-captioning and other accessibility features if the authoring tool makes it available.

Video components of a distributed learning class can be equally frustrating for students. Videos from social media sites like *YouTube* or *Vimeo* may appear to be easy way around setting up a media server. These solutions have potential down sides. The URL can change unexpectedly, or the publisher can change the content. These services also process the video, so there is going to be some degradation of quality from the original.

Students get frustrated when they click "play" and the video is poor or grainy, or their media player suddenly displays a pop-up box asking them to install a new video codec. Students pick up quickly on videos that are dated as well. With the ease of creating high-definition quality video and the readiness of cheap editing tools – training managers should consider creating videos unique to the training program.

Some other tips about video:

1. Use a script.
2. Shoot raw video in the highest definition possible, and keep the raw video files intact in training center library. Always edit copies.
3. Keep segments short. Short segments are easier to edit, are smaller in size, and are easier to get right in fewer "takes".
4. If doing a screen recording, control mouse movement carefully. Edit out delays in transition between screens.
5. Know the types of devices that will be playing the finished video. Scale the video during editing. Frame rates should always be 24 fps or higher (29.97 fps is the US standard).
6. Used closed caption or titling to illustrate key points.

## Mistake 3: Time and Engagement Issues

One positive attribute of distributed learning is that a complex, lengthy course can be rapidly broken into manageable sessions. There are a number of papers that make recommendations on the proper length of an e-learning course. The best answer is not exact - simply, as long as the class keeps the learner engaged. Some research suggests that learners can only pay close attention for as little as 10 minutes.

What keeps learners engaged?

1. Video clips, typically under 5-7 minutes each.
2. Interactive exercises that provide immediate feedback.
3. Self-guided sections, where the learner decides how to proceed through the content.
4. Photos and graphical representations; including those that allow user interaction (hotspots, exploding diagrams, etc.)
5. Animations
6. Questions or quizzes

As a training manager, ensure those tasked with developing distributed learning courses keep the audience engaged. Any content should be specific to the class or course. Discourage the use of stock photography, clip art, or stock animations whenever possible.

## Mistake 4: Feature and Content Overloading

Each authoring tool has its own unique set of features, and the vendors are constantly creating new ways to help training professionals deliver a message. The ever-present technology imperative is lurking in vendor ads and conference presentations: the technology exists therefore we must (a) have it and (b) use it.

Creating learner engagement is a core concept in e-learning development. Many of the 'features' of today's authoring tools focus on these elements. The key to using features is to identify where they have educational value, and are not just stuck into a course because content fit the feature and context.

For example, Adobe Captivate 6 includes no less than ten interaction types, sixteen object types and over 100 effects that can applied to those objects. Designers can easily get lost in the feature set, trying to engage the student with animations and objects rather than the actual curriculum content. Students benefit most when material is presented in a structured manner using a consistent template, with interactions and features being used to make key information stand out.

The same principles apply when an instructional designer tries to deliver too much content in the duration of the class. Not to be confused with classes that are too long or too short, which we just covered. In a short class, it may reasonable to only achieve one outcome. A training manager has to be constantly aware of this, and be a guardian between designers and students.

## Mistake 5: Lack of Evaluation

One of the biggest mistakes that can be made with a distributed learning class is to make it available, and then never follow up with students. Many systems used to deliver e-learning content will support surveys or exams. Especially with the first few participants, go beyond the traditional evaluation. Specifically look for technical problems; sometimes students are reluctant to point out flaws unless specifically asked. Good questions during any pilot testing or course roll-out include:

1. Did you have any issues gaining access to the class once you were registered and received instructions?
2. How long did the class materials take to load?
3. Did you experience any technical issues during the class?
4. How was the audio in the class?
5. What equipment were you using? a mobile device? a laptop?

After a sufficient number of students have participated and provided basic feedback, conduct a class review. See if the e-learning class is comparable to previously offered instructor-led class. Inquire about job performance of both sets.

E-learning is not create, post and forget. One benefit of e-learning is the ability to modify content without having to redistribute materials or retrain instructors. Take advantage of the tools available, and don't be afraid of mistakes - correct them.

## Rapid Development of E-Learning Content

Whether in response to a change in laws or simply arising from the need to improve a specific business practice, the ability to rapidly create e-learning content can challenge even the best training manager. There are five steps that help overcome the challenges of rapid e-learning development. Great e-learning cannot be created overnight, but some simple steps can make the process rapid and relatively painless.

## Use an Advisory Group

One of the best assets a training manager can have is a trusted circle of advisers. An advisory group is very similar to a peer review group, only the scope tends to be broader. A peer review group typically has a focused, narrow topic area. Some of the members may be the same; in other training centers a single group might serve both purposes. The name, structure, and relationship of the group are up to the training center.

Any advisory group must be kept reasonably up-to-date on the training center and its place in the overall business model. This group should be well informed enough that no more than a quick phone call or e-mail is all that is needed to get them engaged in a rapid development situation.

Consider using the advisory group to help establish the purpose and set the initial parameters or requirements for the course. If advisory group members are knowledgeable in the subject matter, consider working with them to develop or review the highest level student learning outcomes. As development and design progresses, this group should serve as the check and balance to the rest of the creative team.

## Set Standards and Build Reusable Components

One of a training center's best tools for rapid e-learning development is a library of components and assets.

- Develop consistent messages and themes for courses. This would include standardized color sets. Use Pantone™, RGB, or hexadecimal color values. Create a logo size, style and usage guide. Generate a library of common visual elements.
- Create templates for common authoring platforms. Identify components that must be consistent with the message and branding, as well as areas where developers can have freedom.
- Identify specific standards for audio and video production (codecs, size, frame rate, etc.). Establish guidelines for titles, credits, overlays, intros and cuts.
- Make use the content library.
- Encourage the creative staff to take "extra" unedited photographs and video. Include these in the library. If using contract video production, be sure to obtain all "b-roll" footage for the project. A photo or video that seems irrelevant to the original project can prove invaluable at a later date.

Simply developing the desired outcomes and establishing proper structure take time. Having templates, clear guidelines, and a well-developed library can greatly reduce the overall development time.

*Maintain Focus & Avoid Scope Creep*

When faced with rapid e-learning development, "scope creep" is a huge threat to the schedule. Scope creep is defined as uncontrolled growth in a project's requirements or capabilities with no corresponding change in resources or schedule. Essentially, scope creep has occurred when a project gets larger than necessary to meet the original purpose. (Wideman, 2012).

As stakeholders review training materials and documents, each will have comments or feedback. Reviewers tend to add to content, and are generally fearful of deleting. With each level of review and comment the content will grow. This is where an advisory or peer review group becomes crucial. By involving the group early in the process and clearly defining the project, it can keep focus on the purpose of the project and limit the scope. Some considerations to minimize scope creep:

- Be sure the purpose of the program is clearly understood.
- Understand the priorities of the training program.
- Define the deliverables related to the program.
- Break the deliverables into actual work requirements.
- Break the project down into major and minor milestones and be aware of the schedule.
- Expect a limited amount of scope creep in every project.
  (Cutting, 2006) (Doll, 2001)

*Leverage Institutional Knowledge / Assets*

Institutional memory is the collective set of facts, concepts, experiences and know-how held by a group of people. Institutional memory becomes institutional knowledge when that collective information is placed into use. An organization requires the ongoing transmission of these memories between members of this group. Institutional memory influences the organizational identity, the association of individuals, and actions of Individuals when interacting with the institution.

"Who in the company knows this topic best?" Training managers often fail to leverage institutional knowledge effectively. Once the purpose and scope of a course is identified, take a moment to identify any internal subject matter experts. If the course is related to a skill, capture experienced personnel on video performing the skill. Use company personnel to explain tasks and provide background on why the task is important.

Using company personnel in photographs and videos provide instant credibility of the information. Using people that are known to and respected by students helps reduce or eliminate obstacles to the training.

*Consider Task-Level Outsourcing*

Consider outsourcing task-level items that require a rapid turnaround. Availability, efficiency and professionalism of resources can make outsourcing an attractive option, especially when company resources have non-training responsibilities. Joe in accounting may have a great voice and do a great job narrating the course, but how long will it take and who will perform his job duties while he is completing this task? Will he be narrating it on his home computer's built-in microphone? The need for speed, efficiency and quality of the finished product make outsourcing a specific assignment a very reasonable course of action.

Tasks that are ideal for outsourcing include:

- Narration / voice-over work
- Graphic design or preparation of custom visual elements
- Video production and post-production
- Development of custom interactive elements (Adobe Flash, JavaScript, etc.)
- Test or evaluation item writing

Identify potential sources and work with them for less urgent projects. Vendors are more inclined to accommodate a rapid turnaround when they have an established relationship. Working with an established vendor also ensures a better understanding of the training center's needs and requirements.

Rapid e-learning development depends largely on the steps taken each day as a training manager or instructional designer. Having an up-to-speed group of advisers, a rich library of assets, and an awareness of institutional knowledge greatly speeds content development for all projects, not just those that require rapid turnarounds.

## Applying Technology

Technology is a major factor in today's training world. Identify and implement technologies that support the growth and development of the student and of the organization's business goals, while avoiding those technologies that are limited in scope or fail to add measurable value.

# THE RIGHT ENVIRONMENT

The training environment consists more of classrooms and tables. Certainly, the physical environment plays a huge role in whether training is successful. Environment includes establishing the correct frame of mind as well. Synonyms for the term *environment* provide a reference to ensure a proper setting for training.

- Location
- Surroundings
- Situation
- Atmosphere

Not every learning activity, and subsequently not every learning environment, will be similar. As with selecting curriculum elements, the key is to tailor the environment in ways that help a student meet the expected student learning outcomes.

## Location

Selecting a location for a training session is rarely as easy as it seems. Some coordinators are lucky enough to have permanent teaching facilities; others either teach at a client's facility or have to find suitable space.

### City & State

If conducting training at a remote location, think carefully about the actual city and state. Training sessions in the winter months can be attractive schedule-wise, but weather can wreak havoc on attendee travel even if the site is a year-round location. Even though the training is scheduled for a California location, attendees coming through Chicago or Philadelphia could easily encounter difficulties. Training in year-round locations can be more expensive because winter is the busy time of year. Think about the driving distance and cost for potential students. Consider the diversity of lodging and eating establishments. Know the audience and try to match with a city having a range of prices and amenities suitable for their income and background.

**College towns can be an excellent option for conducting training during summer months.**

When considering a city and state, also consider the costs associated with production (Audio-visual equipment rental, staging, lighting, etc.) and moving training materials to the remote location. People have become accustomed to being able to ship overnight. Delivery and shipping companies are vulnerable to weather and travel disruptions also, and being caught without critical training materials can be a huge problem.

## Training Site

There are always options when it comes to selecting the building and room(s) for training. Often, coordinators get locked into a particular site even when if not the best selection. Training room selection often comes down to what is available, or what is free. Remember the old cliché though; the buyer gets what is paid for. Sometimes a small investment in a hotel conference room can have a huge impact. The type of training being delivered comes into play also; great classroom facilities at a hotel may not be a factor if the class involves a hands-on skill. Potential locations can be local colleges, community rooms at fire or police stations, and hotels. A local for-profit training center may even be willing to barter facilities for goods or services.

Sometimes trainers feel an imperative to teach at a specific location; such as conducting a session for athletic trainers at a sports venue. Coordinators should not feel tied to a specific location unless that location truly benefits the students. If a program consists of classroom component, uses easily moved props or materials, and can be done inside – students may appreciate finding a better location than a team locker room with benches. On the other hand, if the program requires a lot of resources and will take place on the field, the sports facility may be the best choice for that part of the session. A training manager must think carefully about what the student is being asked to learn, and give them the best location possible. Consider creature comforts as well when picking out the site and room. Develop a list of potential sites in the area, and then take a look at the surroundings of each site.

### Case Study: Martinsville Speedway

Martinsville Speedway has a limited infrastructure. Space is at a premium year-round, yet the Speedway's management team needed to conduct annual training for the emergency services staff. Conducting two days of training that combined classroom with skill development and scenario-based exercises for nearly 150 students presented a challenge. With no space suitable for classroom use, the Speedway's Training Coordinator had to be creative. Henry County, Virginia's Public Safety Training Facility was located approximately four miles away, and had multiple classrooms and facilities. The Training Coordinator designed an agenda that allowed for job-related classroom activity in the morning. After lunch, students moved to the Speedway for skills components. The Coordinator used available resources to get the most from available facilities.

### Room Environment Checklist

- ☐ What is the shape of the room? Rooms that are square tend to work best.
- ☐ Does the room appear clean and well-maintained?
- ☐ Is the work space for each student adequate?
  - ○ Does each student have space (allow 3' per student)?
  - ○ Are the chairs comfortable?

- o Does each student seat provide an adequate view of the instructor and presentation?
- o Does each student have secure storage space?
- o Does each student have power / internet access (WiFi code) if needed?
- ☐ Evaluate floors and walls. Floors should be carpeted, and walls free from items that aren't specifically meeting-related. Avoid black and brown painted rooms in favor of warm, pastel-colored rooms when possible.
- ☐ Are the room's environmental controls accessible? If not – who has access?
- ☐ Are the room's lighting controls appropriate for the class?
  - o Can individual lights be turned off selectively to accommodate a presentation?
  - o Can any natural light be blocked out? How does the natural lighting change throughout the day?
- ☐ Are there adequate restroom facilities for the expected student count?
- ☐ Is there a student lounge or similar area, with drinks and snacks for purchase if not provided?
- ☐ Identify potential distractions. Can they be managed or controlled?
- ☐ Check for noise. Potential sources include HVAC systems, from hallways or other rooms, or from outside the building.
- ☐ Are there any safety issues? Pay special attention to stairs.
- ☐ Is the facility compliant with the Americans with Disabilities Act?
- ☐ Is the parking area well lit and safe?

## Surroundings

Once a potential location has been nailed down, consider the area's immediate surroundings. Do thorough research before committing to a specific venue. Are any of the potential sites adjacent to airport arrival and departure patterns? Is there construction going on in the immediate area that will inhibit traffic or create a distraction? What is the traffic situation at/near the site? If unfamiliar with the area, talk with local public safety officials to find out if there are any crime or known issues. All of these can make for an unpleasant student experience.

When working with a site and the training group will not be the only activity at the property that day, find out details of other activities. Are they of a competing nature? Will the other activities present a distraction for students? A coordinator recently hosted a session in a wonderful classroom overlooking an elaborate foyer in a Las Vegas hotel; he had used this location frequently with no issues. The setting had always been an excellent choice. Halfway through the afternoon session, the instructor realized his students were intently watching a celebrity wedding in the foyer. The instructor lacked any method of blocking the student's view.

One resource a training manager should maintain a relationship with is the convention and visitor's bureau. Smaller towns may have an economic development office or

Chamber of Commerce serving a similar function. Look at other events and facilities in the area and try to determine if any of their activities will impact training.

## Situation

Creating the right situation for learning to occur is the point at which a training manager crosses over from purely logistical concerns to creating synergy. Synergy between the location, students, curriculum, and trainer greatly improves transfer of training. Setting up the proper situation begins with understanding the needs assessment that led to the training. Why is this training occurring? What do is known about the audience? Establishing the right situation is where the training manager applies knowledge of the audience.

As a training manager, some training schedules may come with a very negative audience. Use changes in the environment to counter an anticipated negative environment. If past classes have been taught in a company break room, consider moving the class to the board room or off-site. Provide food and beverage. Coffee and doughnuts before an early morning session can help create a more positive situation for the instructor. If the material has been taught by the same instructor, consider using a different trainer or encourage a different instructional method.

---

**Two proven ways to improve the morale and attitude of a class are to offer food and freebies.**

---

Training managers can improve the situation is to improve the status of the program in the student's eyes. Telling students that a program is important generally has little impact. Having the president of the company or a relevant outside speaker introduce the training session not only improves credibility, but carries the unspoken message that training is important. Such messaging is especially impactful if the training occurs during "off hour" times or on weekends. The company president showing up on Sunday morning at 7:00 AM to introduce a training session can make a valuable statement about the importance of a training program.

---

**If a special guest or executive is planning an appearance, let the appearance be a surprise if possible.**

---

There are other ways a training manager can manipulate the situation and environment in favor of learning:

- Ensure paper and pen or pencils are positioned at each student's seat.
- Place a business card from each instructor for each student.
- Place the day's agenda, along with a list of expected student learning outcomes, for each student.
- Have instructors dress similarly for the day. Students appreciate being able to rapidly identify staff members.

- Depending on the class, use name cards at their seat or name tags for all participants. This is especially important if the student is paying a fee for a class.

## Atmosphere

Establishing the correct atmosphere once training begins is equally important. Making the effort in the areas of location, surrounding and situation helps ensure a good environment. A training manager's hard work can be undone easily by a single instructor bringing a negative tone to class.

### When Students Arrive

What do students see when they first arrive at training? As the cliché goes, there is no second chance to make a first impression. Do they see an instructor rushing to set up? How are the instructor(s) dressed? Ensure any sign-in or registration processes are rehearsed and run smoothly. Avoid creating long lines of people just waiting to get in the door! Was there a member of the instructional staff assigned as a greeter and to answer student questions as they arrive?

Tips on facilitating student arrival:

- Use signage liberally. Message boards (easel signs, sandwich boards) that use either a large dry-erase or changeable letter surface area generally cost under $200 and can be great for directing traffic into a particular entrance or parking area. Be sure each room or location has signage that matches the agenda or location map provided to students.
- Use a pre-registration process to minimize the need for students to fill out forms and documents. Use alphabetized, pre-printed sign-in sheets if a signature is required. Limit 'paperwork' done during class to documents that require a real signature.
- If any part of the registration process requires a student interact one-on-one with a staff member (such as taking ID photos or reviewing an employment agreement) use a sign-in sheet then call the students individually.
- Ensure training staff members are easily identified, either through clothing or name badges.
- If training is being conducted at a specific location on a large facility, be sure other departments are aware of the training activity and location so that students can be directed to the proper location. This is especially true of the security personnel or main reception desk staff.
- All equipment, including A/V components, should be set up and turned on prior to any student entering the training area.
- Consider playing a relevant video from the time the doors open until the start of the session. Be sure to obtain permission for public display of the material from the copyright holder if not produced by the training center. Alternatively, display an available television channel of common interest.

The first instructor to speak at the beginning of the session has a huge responsibility. What he or she says, the demeanor, and even body language establishes the atmosphere for a class. Think about a favorite television show or movie – how does the first few moments of the show draw viewers in?

Starting a class is very much like any other public speaking opportunity. The first few moments are critical, and the training manager or other opening speaker has four main objectives within the first five minutes of a class:

1. Get the attention and interest of the class.
2. Reinforce the topic of the class.
3. Establish credibility and goodwill.
4. Preview the remainder of the session. (Lucas, 2009)

## Getting Attention

Grabbing the attention of students can be difficult, especially when the topic is well known. Professional speakers use a variety of techniques. (Lucas, 2009)

- Establish relevance and importance to the students.
- Startle the students.
- Make students curious.
- Question the students' ideas or beliefs.
- Begin with a quotation or introductory clip from an important figure.
- Tell a story that utilizes these one or more techniques.

Negative statements undermine the planning and effort the training staff has put into establishing the right situation needed for learning to occur. Every individual speaking at the introduction to a training activity should be positive, even if doing so means speaking from prepared remarks or notes.

---

**Stay positive. Once an instructor sets a negative tone, the damage is done.**

---

## Avoid Time-Wasting Icebreakers

Fledgling trainers are routinely taught to use *icebreakers* at the start of class. Many icebreakers are characterized as team-building methods, get acquainted activities, or just plain fun tasks. Icebreakers are facilitation exercises, often involving the sharing of personal information. Instructors are told to use these techniques to break down barriers and open individuals up to the training process.

The corporate training environment is different. Corporate training exists to support profitable business activities – training affects production and carries a significant cost when done correctly. So what would a CEO or shareholder think if they stopped to greet the class and found them playing the M & M Game? The M & M Game involves students standing six feet apart and tossing candy at a partner's mouth in response to questions, often of a personal nature. A prize is typically given to the winner.

---

**Traditional icebreakers are not appropriate for most workplace training programs.**

---

In workplace training, time is valuable. Work flow may be slowed or stopped. The company may be paying for coverage or overtime. Even in large companies, many training attendees already know each other. They may share information on a social network, or live in the same neighborhood.

To help instructors, the training manager should be creative and help instructors find creative yet functional ways to start a workplace class. These methods won't be embarrassing if a CEO walks in, yet are still engaging.

### Example 1: I Rely On

This exercise is a great way to start the dreaded "required" training classes. Have each student identify and thank a person in the room whom he or she relies on. To really tie the statement together, have the student comment on why the training is important to the person being relied on. This helps create a very real link between training and the work environment. The exercise is brief and requires no resources.

> Jim and Jean work on a manufacturing line together, and are attending a required CPR/First Aid class. "I'm Jim, and I rely on Jean to monitor the product put out by my machine. It's important for her to know first aid because if anything happens to four of us operating these machines, she is the person most available to provide immediate assistance."

### Example 2: We Made This

If individuals are from unlike departments (i.e., marketing and manufacturing), consider this exercise. Bring a sample or two of the company's product. Each student states how he or she contributed to the customer's purchase of the product. Note that students should not focus on the manufacture of the product itself; focus on the end result - a sold product. Similar to the first exercise, have the student provide a direct link between the training and his or her job responsibility. Again, this activity takes very little time and requires only a product sample.

> Jose works in accounting for a furniture manufacturing company. A small table made by the company is on display at the front of the room. "I'm Jose, and I am responsible for paying the bills to our wood supplier and ensuring we get our materials at the most favorable pricing."

### Example 3: I Want To Teach

Every company has a river of institutional knowledge that runs through the employee base. Although a training manager may tap into these resources from time to time, many go unnoticed. Each student should identify a topic he or she would like to teach and explain why the class would benefit the company. Ask a follow-up question or two if needed to understand why the topic is important both to the individual and the company. This information should be captured and considered as part of the training center's needs assessment. An individual that presents a thorough, articulate picture may be a great future instructor.

> Gina works as an administrative assistant and travel coordinator. "I'm Gina, and I want to teach a class in our time clock procedure for managers. This class is really needed, because I spend five hours each week fixing the same set of errors. I know our system isn't the most efficient, but there are some tips I've learned that will actually make the process simpler for them."

One of the biggest reasons to take control of icebreakers or similar activities is out of respect for time – both the company's and the students'.

## Time

Time is a huge component of keeping the right atmosphere. One of the fastest ways to a positive class evaluation is to manage time properly. Managing time shows respect for the student's investment in the class – especially if the class occurs on a day off or in non-traditional hours.

- Start and end the class on time. Instructors often think ending a class early is acceptable. As a training manager, an instructor dismissing early means that either the curriculum needs modifying, or that the instructor failed to cover the curriculum as designed.
- Avoid going more than 15 minutes off schedule during the day.
- Consider the program's time footprint – are students driving in from a distance? Don't set class times so that students have to travel early in the morning or late at night. A student that arrives at class exhausted cannot participate fully.
- Instructors should never talk longer than a student's chair can remain comfortable.
- Avoid "all classroom" days whenever possible; use hands-on or interactive elements to break up the day.

Think about this scenario: a student calls the lead instructor fifteen minutes before class is to start, saying he will be ten minutes late for class. Should the instructor delay the start of class for a single student? What message does this send to the students that arrived on time?

If the training consists of multiple sessions going on at the same time, appoint a single individual as the schedule master. This person is assigned the responsibility for keeping multiple groups and instructors on time. Use a public address system or radio system to give pre-emptive announcements (10 minutes left, time to switch).

# The Role of the CEO in Training

Has the CEO or senior management team been asked to get involved in training? Before lamenting the absence of management support, a training manager should take a direct approach and ask them to get involved. A CEO's involvement dramatically affects the training environment.

> ### Case Study: The Surprise CEO
>
> A rather large facility was conducting orientation for a group of new hospitality employees early on a Saturday morning. The training manager prepared an excellent agenda and instructional program. The CEO of the facility, in his office working on other projects, noticed the flurry of incoming vehicles and people. Curious, he sought out the source of the activity. The training manager was shocked when the CEO showed up, and even more shocked when he pulled out a chair and stayed for most of the class. Afterwards, his remarks to the training manager were candid; the CEO's view was that the hospitality staff was a customer's direct point of contact. Therefore, every hospitality employee has a direct relationship with his responsibilities. Prior to the session, the CEO was aware of training but the opportunity to get involved had not been present. The relationship between the training manager and CEO improved dramatically after the session, and the CEO was a constant presence at training activities.

Senior managers and chief executives should take on a variety of responsibilities in support of the training function. Corporate leaders that embrace these responsibilities create a positive learning environment and a true culture of learning within the company. The management team has five core responsibilities to setting up the right environment:

1. Vision
2. Sponsorship
3. Governance
4. Participation
5. Representation

## Vision

---

**The CEO provides a vision for the impact of training on the organization.**

---

The CEO has to provide general direction for the training function, which helps establish the environment within which the training manager works and all training occurs. This goes beyond the typical mission/vision statement rhetoric. A vision does not mean "I want the training department to..." Vision is the CEO's expression of what the true culture of the organization should be with regard to training, education, and overall improvement of the people within the company. Jack Welch, former CEO of General Electric (GE), had a vision to transform the company using the Six Sigma model. Welch's vision was for every employee to be trained in the process and have responsibility for at least one project. His $500 million investment had a 100% return on investment in four years. (Meister, 2000). The CEO has to not only have a vision, but also clearly articulate it so that the vision can be implemented successfully.

## Sponsorship

---
**The CEO ensures the training center has sufficient resources.**

---

Training requires resources and people. Establishing a good training environment requires funding. A sponsor, by definition, provides funding for something they support. The CEO or senior management team fills the sponsor role when they provide financial support for the training department. The sponsor is the training center's advocate within the boardroom when necessary, ensuring that the vision can move forward.

## Governance

---
**The CEO is involved in strategy and planning.**

---

The CEO's role as a governor of the training center means they should be active in strategy and planning without falling into a trap of micromanagement. If the training manager can be describe as principal of the corporate "school", the CEO could be described as the county manager. The training manager is in place to do the heavy lifting and execution of the plan. Some CEO's implement a governing board to provide guidance for the training function. Others choose to be directly involved. One of the basic functions of a training center is to identify opportunities for training in support the larger business goals. The CEO is best suited to help ensure the training center fills this need.

Governance isn't a one-way street. The training center benefits greatly from having a direct relationship with the CEO. Just like the head of a state transportation or education department has access to the governor to intervene and assist with problems, the training manager has a direct method to bypass complex corporate bureaucracies. The CEO has knowledge of the entire organization, and can provide a wealth of insight and direction. Even if informal in nature, the CEO and training manager should have regular conversations.

## Participation

---
**The CEO is a subject matter expert, a teacher, and a student.**

---

Many training managers believe the CEO has too many other responsibilities to be an active participant in training. In many successful companies, that isn't the case. GE's Jack Welch routinely taught classes twice a month at GE's corporate university. CEO's can play an active role in the training center as a subject matter expert, teacher and student.  In Meister's review of seven companies, the one role that all seven CEO's shared was that of an active participant in actual training. (Meister, 2000).

The CEO has significant knowledge gained from current and previous roles.  That knowledge should be tapped as the training center develops programs and materials.  The CEO isn't required to be a member of the development group, although he or she certainly can be. Participation as a subject matter expert can come through reviewing final drafts of course materials, or a video cameo explaining why the topic is important to the company.  Perhaps one of the most significant expressions that a topic is important is when the CEO takes the reigns in the classroom as an instructor.  Especially in a larger company, the CEO's interaction with both the training center and other employees is a great opportunity for feedback.

### Representation

---

**The CEO is the face and voice of training for the organization.**

---

The CEO is often the public face of the company or brand. The CEO should also be the face and voice of training both within the organization and publicly.  During GE's transformation, the company and Jack Welch became known prominently for both training initiatives and product lines.  GE remains consistently ranked in the top ten of many "best places" lists, with training cited as a factor for many of those selections. (Meister, 2000).

When a CEO is asked to contribute to a publication, or be interviewed, that's an opportunity to promote a vision for the company and training's role.  The CEO should ensure that information on training is included in the annual corporate report. Encouraging other members of senior management to get involved in training is also part of the CEO's role as training's chief marketer.

Not every CEO will take an active role in training, despite the benefits to the training environment.  Look for opportunities to engage other members of the senior management team without abandoning the organizational structure.

## Outdoor Training

There are many skills that require a trainee to do skills demonstrations or scenario-based training outside.  These training evolutions present a wide range of challenges for a training manager.  An outdoor setting makes management of the training environment extremely difficult.

### Logistics

Logistical concerns are a top priority when planning an outdoor training session.

- How will students move from one location to another? Allowing students to use their own vehicles may be ok, but consider the implications if there is a collision during training. Often the easiest way is by passenger van, bus or tram with an operator who is approved by the vehicle and/or property owner. Walking is rarely a good answer to the movement question, as students become distracted and wander.
- If teaching skills at a remote location how will breaks and bathroom issues be handled? Consider the use of portable toilets, or allow time in the agenda for transportation to/from the common area. If using portable toilets, consider having separate units for male and female students – a little courtesy pays huge dividends. If portable toilets are impractical, consider having a training team member assigned to a vehicle or cart to ferry students requiring the use of facilities.
- Communications between instructors and organizers can be challenging; consider the use of two-way radios to avoid constant use of a mobile phone.
- Ensure that appropriate safety resources are available and that all instructors know the procedures in the event of an emergency. Know where first aid kits and material safety data sheets are located.
- Keep student groups small and active during observation, demonstration, and practice. Students that are waiting in line develop a negative attitude quickly; plan adequate resources and staff to keep students busy.
- If skills are being taught in close proximity to each other, use temporary fencing or other barrier structures to keep groups from mingling together or becoming distracted. Providing educational distractions keeps students from finding one of their own.

## Weather

A training manager has to consider the weather forecast in the same breath as logistics. There truly is no such thing as "perfect weather" for outdoor training. Here are some points to consider related to the weather:

- Review the weather forecast at 10, 7, and 3 days out. Distribute weather forecasts to the training staff and students.
- Develop a range of "weather plans" based on the high temperature, low temperature, precipitation type and probability, wind, and severe weather possibilities.
- If the air temperature will be above 80 degrees Fahrenheit, consider it a hot day. Plan for plenty of shade in skill areas, using tents if air-conditioned space isn't available nearby. Keep coolers of bottled water or sports drinks on hand at each station.
- If the air temperature will be below 65 degrees Fahrenheit, consider it a cold day and plan accordingly.

- Remember that the student audience may have a different perception of hot or cold than the instructor. For example, students from Florida will perceive a 60° F day differently than a student from Quebec, Canada.
- If severe weather is a concern, create a plan and share it with instructors. Know safe shelter locations and emergency signals.
- Purchase a lightning detector; versions are available for under $100. If an individual is assigned to monitor the schedule and serve as a central point of communication, provide the detector to that individual.
- Understand how temperature and wind extremes can affect equipment and props. Be sure all instructors understand the parameters of safe operation, and how to act when those parameters are exceeded.

### Realism

One of the main reasons coordinators choose to train outdoors is to foster realism during skills or scenario-based training. Choosing to do this type of training can be very effective, but also very costly. Training managers have to ensure that the training ground is used efficiently to get the maximum return on investment. Plan to create the most realistic environment possible, within the parameters of safety, efficiency / student throughput, and budget.

- Extreme realism can significantly extend the amount of time needed to reset props and tools between groups. Plan to have multiple activities set up, and use support or logistics personnel reset props while instructors continue moving students through evolutions.
- Simulating, or simply "talking through" elements of a scenario or skill defeats the purpose of setting up a realistic situation. Allow plenty of time for each group to actually perform the necessary skills.
- Students learn hands-on skills through repetition. Simply performing a skill once, then undergoing a critique and moving to another station sets the student up for failure. Use skills stations and scenarios to allow students to practice multiple times, with plenty of opportunity for feedback from the training staff between efforts.

## Being Prepared

Despite the best planning and preparations, situations will arise that are outside the training manager's control. Overcoming challenges and maintaining a quality learning environment often relies on a real diligence in planning. Audio-visual equipment that worked perfectly yesterday, will fail right as class starts. Wonderfully planned outdoor skills stations are in place until Mother Nature serves up a round of lightning and severe storms.

Students don't really care why things don't go as planned. Most students don't really care how much a class deviates from the original plan. Students want a quality learning experience. They want to learn something new, or learn how to do something better.

There are four basic rules for preparation a training manager should consider:

- All Audio-Visual equipment, including the internet connection, will fail. In addition to a backup, have a plans for training without the Internet, without power, without a projector, and without a computer.
- Always assume the weather will be severe – plan for wind, rain, snow, and lightning; remember that weather affects everyone's ability to travel.
- Twice the planned number of students will show up, but only half of the planned instructors.
- Have a backup plan for every element of the day and every piece of equipment.

Invariably, every training session will have challenges. How the training manager and staff respond to the challenge is what students remember. In an ideal situation, the students are not even aware of the problem. Knowing about a problem, not acknowledging the issue, and pushing forward with a bad plan can lead to a training disaster. Even when faced with that "perfect storm" of training problems, the training manager has a responsibility to the organization and students. Give students a 10-minute break, bring the training team together, and come up with a plan. Communicate the plan and execute it. Students will forgive early challenges and the unplanned break if they come back to a valuable learning session.

When things don't go as planned, be honest with students and staff. Take ownership of the issues and the resolution. Avoid any perception of passing the buck or blaming others. Acknowledge the fact there were challenges, and commit to providing the best program possible under those circumstances. Everyone will appreciate the candor and honesty; they will also recognize and appreciate the training staff going "the extra mile" to ensure the success of the program. Expect things to go wrong, and plan options.

# THE RIGHT INSTRUCTORS

Getting the right person to deliver content is critical. Not every instructor is suited to teach every subject; an instructor can be much more effective when allowed to focus on topics within a given scope. Every training organization must also have solid "utilitarian" instructors that can be called on to teach a variety of topics on short notice.

Even with the shift of curricula to distributed learning the need for instructor involvement continues. Current estimates show about 28% of learning takes place online or in a virtual classroom. (American Society for Training & Development, 2011). Good instructors must deliver content that was previously delivered in the classroom using new methods, and be able to interact with students online. The abilities to provide advice by e-mail and guide discussion boards are essential skills.

Identifying and developing good instructors is a priority for every training manager. Documenting the screening process, monitoring, and ongoing evaluation of each instructor is a good habit. As with the curriculum, establishing a peer or stakeholder group to provide feedback can prove very helpful.

Instructors are often thought of in global terms – as an instructor for the training organization. The best training managers think of instructors as a resource to be utilized. Instructors can be assigned to a curriculum, to a specific class, or even to specific sections of a single class.

**IMPORTANT NOTE:**
The process for selecting instructors varies widely. In some organizations, instructors may be employees, outside contractors or volunteers. Because the role of the instructor is closely related to the training entity, consult with both human resources personnel and legal counsel on the instructor selection and monitoring processes.

## Understanding Instructor Traits

Training managers are responsible for instructor performance in the corporate training center. Whether a training organization calls these people trainers, instructors, educators, or faculty, good instructors all share common traits.

- Experience and expertise
- Professionalism
- Enthusiasm and motivation
- Leadership
- Instructional ability
- Technological ability

### Experience / Expertise

Identifying individuals with appropriate experience may seem easy to quantify and validate. An instructor's resume is a good starting point. Is the training center looking for experience or expertise? On the surface that difference may seem a bit trivial, but when it comes to transfer of training it can be crucial.

*Experience* can be defined as exposure to a broad range of experiences in a given field, typically over a period of time. When looking for experience, consider what the person's scope of decision making and responsibility have been. Before screening a single instructor, ask the peer group what type and length of experiences would be most valuable to the program.

*Expertise* can perhaps be defined as a very deep knowledge of a specific topic or area. Expertise can be gained through education, experience, and many other mechanisms. Unlike experience, expertise may not be related to time in a single position or function. The peer group can also identify specific expertise of value to the program and students.

Remember that the length of someone's experience is not all that matters; the quality and frequency with which the potential instructor performs a specific task is equally significant. A person that performs a task once a year for three years is less experienced than the person performing the task weekly for six months.

### Professionalism

Professionalism is a broad term, often with a positive connotation. So what defines professionalism in a corporate instructor?

- They smile, have a positive attitude, and say "Thank You" frequently.
- They praise their mentors, peers and students – not themselves.
- They constantly share their knowledge in both formal and informal environments.
- A professional communicates effectively, remembering to focus on what is meant and what is heard by the receiver – not what is said. A professional has mastered the art of listening.
- A professional often does more than what is required or what is expected.
- They adhere to high values and principles; are punctual; dress properly; exhibit honesty and fairness; have high ethical and moral standards; and use good manners and proper etiquette.
- They place the task of helping students reach the desired outcome(s) as their top priority. (Norton, 2010)

In many ways, professionalism is synonymous with the "face" of the training organization. Just as the training manager can select images and media elements for the training mateirals, instructors should be selected that present the correct professional presence to students.

## Enthusiasm & Motivation

Enthusiasm is contagious. A properly motivated, enthusiastic instructor can have a huge impact on virtually any program. But simply appearing energetic and enthusiastic isn't enough. The best instructors can clearly communicate 'why' they are enthusiastic and motivated in a way that touches the student.

Each instructor candidate should be prepared to answer the question "why is teaching this particular program important to you?" Understanding what motivates an individual to teach a specific program can give the training manager valuable insight. In addition to knowledge, skills and abilities – the instructor often transfers some of their own personal motivation to the student population. Look for motives that are consistent with the values of the curriculum and the training organization.

An important but often overlooked aspect of selecting the right individuals to teach a program is the dynamic between instructors. Students that move from an outgoing, highly motivated instructor will face challenges if their subsequent instructor is equally knowledgeable but quiet and less expressive.

## Leadership

Dr. Stephen R. Covey defines a great leader as someone who communicates to people their worth and potential so clearly that they are inspired to see it in themselves. His definition makes it clear why leadership is an important quality of the right instructor. How can instructor candidates with leadership potential be identified?

First, recognize that leadership and the decision to become an instructor is a choice. Individuals who are pressured into becoming an instructor rarely perform at an equal level to an individual who chooses to teach.

Beyond that initial step, look for individuals that:

- Inspire trust
- Clarify purpose
- Align systems and ideas
- Unleash talent

Evaluating these qualities in a potential instructor can be difficult. One telling indication of a top-tier instructor is when a number of former students have gone on to become instructors themselves.

### Instructional Ability

Instructional ability could be considered the technical component of an instructor. What kind of abilities has the instructor developed, either from past teaching assignments or past experience? An instructor has to take on a variety of roles or characteristics throughout the delivery of a program.

| Possible Instructor Roles | | | |
|---|---|---|---|
| Taskmaster | Salesperson | Cheerleader | Critic |
| Mentor | Administrator | Friend | Moderator |
| Peer | Authoritarian | Entertainer | Judge |
| Evaluator | Supervisor | Expert | Logistics |
| Guide | Explorer | Resource | Architect |
| Safety Officer | Public Relations | Clerical Staff | Research Analyst |

Based on the curriculum, a few of these roles may have greater significance. Use the analysis of the instructor candidate's experience and expertise to correlate characteristics with ability and needs of the individual topic. There are some basic characteristics that are often cited:

- Is the individual knowledgeable of the topic?
- Does the individual communicate effectively?
- Do they understand the learning process as it applies to the intended audience?
- Is the individual perceptive and adaptive to the audience?
- Is the individual committed to the audience both as a whole, and as individuals?

### Technological Ability

As distributed learning technology continues to expand in corporate training, an instructor's ability to understand and utilize technology becomes more important each year. Gauging an instructor's ability to use classroom technologies effectively can be very difficult. Some instructors are exceptional at setting up and delivering realistic scenarios in a hands-on program, yet struggle to set up a classroom's audio and video.

Be honest in an assessment of the technology needs associated with a curriculum and its components. Develop a 'technology tool' for each course element identifying the technology required and anticipating the challenges an instructor can face. This information is important in the instructor selection process.

## The Instructor Career Cycle

There has been a lot of research into how the concept of a career has changed with each generation. Although no clear definition has been agreed upon by experts, the training manager has to understand instructors will pass through three distinct phases in their career. (Noe, 2010). Instructor phases include the apprentice, the colleague, and the mentor. These phases do not correlate with specific titles or roles. Instead, they match with the instructional experience and position within the career cycle.

### Exploration – The Apprentice

Most new instructors are explorers. Explorers have time on the job – typically a couple of years, but tend to be younger. These individuals often seek to become instructors out of interest in a specific subject matter, and can be highly motivated. They may need help and direction from more seasoned instructors at times.

Often instructor status is seen as a method of standing out from other employees in hope of advancement or status. These instructors are often motivated by the socioeconomic rewards or becoming an instructor. Because they are newer and may be less influenced by existing processes, these instructors are frequently a source of good ideas and feedback.

Instructors at this stage frequently make good hands-on or adjunct instructors. They may not have sufficient expertise to place in the classroom, but have sufficient experience to be effective in the proper situations. .

### Establishment – The Colleague

In the second stage, instructors tend to be slightly older – between 30 and 45, and have experience ranging from 5-10 years on a topic. These individuals typically have a solid mix of experience and expertise. They are usually very engaged with the training center on a number of levels, and interact frequently with other instructors.

As an instructor becomes established, they usually look for ways to make individual contributions to the company, to training, or both. They tend to be less motivated by the financial or status rewards. These instructors are motivated more by the social interaction with other instructors and the desire to be a part of the company's success.

### Maintenance – The Mentor

An instructor that reaches the mentoring stage tends to be slightly older, having gained 10 or more years' experience as an instructor. These instructors tend to have the most experience and expertise. Their understanding of the company, the training center, and daily operations make them an excellent source of institutional knowledge.

Instructors that grow to the mentoring stage have a unique challenge – staying relevant. Many instructors at this stage rely on the knowledge and experience they have accrued over their career. Instructors at this level should be encouraged to maintain skills at the highest level.

## Getting and Keeping Quality Instructors

Once a training manager has a good handle on the individual traits as they apply to the training center, the challenge becomes applying that knowledge to match instructors to educational programs.

## Identifying Traits

Each educational program has specific traits that are more relevant or applicable. Good instructional design identifies important traits in curriculum materials. Use a chart to put together a good picture of the ideal instructor for a class.

Identifying the traits unique to a class is a critical step in developing the instructor application. Don't worry about rating the general traits of leadership, motivation, and professionalism when defining class level traits. Those are more easily rated later in the application process as a way of narrowing the applicant list.

### Instructor-Course Assessment Sheet

A simple table and rating structure can help identify skills and abilities an instructor needs to successfully teach a course. An expanded version of this table is available as a Microsoft Word document from the Oak Tree Systems' site: https://www.dropbox.com/sh/z19kxslkjo3hvlg/yzbzGYAycu.

## Course Name:

| Area / Skill<br>What skills or abilities are necessary for an instructor teaching this course? | Required Level<br>1=Low to 5=High |
|---|---|
| **Experience** | |
| | 1  2  3  4  5 |
| | 1  2  3  4  5 |
| | 1  2  3  4  5 |
| | 1  2  3  4  5 |

## Creating an Application Process

Once specific areas or skills are matched with a course, construct an application. One of the principal factors in an instructor's performance is the *desire* to teach a specific topic. Requiring instructors to apply for permission to teach a course validates the instructor's ability and desire to teach.

**Develop a process that matches instructor traits with class needs.**

Using the information from the curriculum and assessment sheet, create an application process that will help identify instructors ideally suited for a class. The process can be simple or complex. Experience and expertise can be assessed in a variety of ways.

*Assessing Expertise and Experience*

### Detailed Application Questions

Asking someone to provide copies of degrees, credentials, or certifications is standard practice. The training manager should develop more detailed questions that evaluate whether the candidate meets the level of experience or expertise required.

For example:  If First Aid Instructor is a required certification, expand upon the request for a copy of the certification document. Ask the candidate "How many students have you taught in the past two years?" or "Describe how a student has used skills taught in an emergency."

## Situational Questions

In addition to the standard statements found in an application, consider asking the candidate to answer situational questions relevant to the curriculum.  Don't be afraid to propose difficult scenarios.

## Knowledge Exam

Although less common today, a knowledge exam can help corroborate a potential expert's statements on the application or resume.  Questions should reflect the level of knowledge the instructor will need to not only teach the topic, but at the depth to answer student questions.

## Abilities Demonstration

Technology allows training managers a greater variety of options for seeing a potential instructor "at work".  Requesting work samples is an acceptable practice – whether asking for a video of the instructor teaching a relevant topic, or asking for submission of a detailed lesson plan.  Web-based conferencing makes it easy and inexpensive to gather a group of potential instructors and conduct a virtual class.

## "On the Job" Evaluation

Dependent upon the program and specific training needs, observing an instructor candidate "on the job" is a valuable method of evaluating experience and expertise.  In addition to information on the candidate's experience and expertise, valuable insight can be gained into the individual's instructional ability.

### *Assessing Professionalism and Other Traits*

Assessing the professionalism of an individual is easiest when a training manager is already familiar with the instructor candidate, perhaps from seeing the candidate "on the job" or as an adjunct instructor for another program.

Consider using a web-based meeting product for a "get acquainted" session with instructor candidates; doing so can provide a better feel for how the instructor candidates will represent the curriculum to students.  Speak to former students and peers; see if they speak with emotion or passion about their experience and interaction with the instructor candidate.

There are many tools available to help training managers evaluate a candidate's instructional ability. Consider simplifying observations based on Gilbert Highet's *The Art of Teaching*.  Highet identified only three basic characteristics to form a simple but effective instructor evaluation:

- Does the person know what they teach?
- Do they like what they teach?
- Do they like their students? (Highet, 1989).

Develop a technology profile of each instructor candidate. Identify technologies found in the training center and ask candidates to self-assess their ability with each. Even if the candidate falls out of the selection process, these skills may be of use in a supporting role.

## Selecting Instructors

Develop standards for each of the application process criteria and compare each instructor candidate to the individual standards. Avoid comparing instructor candidates to each other; focus on each person's ability to bring the student forward to the desired outcome.

---

**Compare instructor candidates to a defined standard, not each other.**

---

Treat the instructor selection process much like an employment process. Instructors are the ones ultimately responsible for delivery of the curriculum and student performance. Selection panels are a common practice; when used they should incorporate a variety of personnel familiar with the planned curriculum.

Some tips for the instructor selection process:

- Always publish an application deadline, and stick to it.
- Acknowledge the receipt of every application.
- Review applications as they are submitted for completeness.
- Consider redacting personal information (such as names, affiliations, etc.) if using a selection panel, to prevent personal bias.
- Although one individual may be assigned to pre-screen applications, always make the entire application pool available to the selection panel.
- Look for individuals that can be good instructors of the course, not just people who meet criteria.

Sometimes the training manager or selection panel needs to have an open mind. An experienced individual with 20 years' experience and a good reputation might deserve an opportunity to be an instructor even if lacking in formal credentials. Developing instructors is a great opportunity to involve members of the organization.

## Train-the-Trainer Programs

Train-the-Trainer programs are a great opportunity to leverage institutional knowledge. Programs can take two forms.

The first form takes an existing group of trainers and introduces them to a new curriculum. Instructors may have limited experience in the area addressed by the curriculum. A significant amount of time may be spent ensuring the instructors have the appropriate knowledge and skill level to teach the material effectively. These instructors have the ability to follow a lesson plan, so spend time building psychomotor skills. Rather than focus on the individual elements of lecture notes, focus on explaining the underlying rationale. The instructors will have the ability to communicate "Do X, then Y". Prepare them for the student question "Why X first?"

In the second common type of train-the-trainer program, individuals with significant institutional knowledge but no training experience are introduced to basic instructor methodology. These individuals may already know how and why a task is performed. These students typically need to work on public speaking and be taught how to coach students during skills sessions. These types of programs are also a great way to get managers or supervisors invested in training.

### Instructor Development

Training managers cannot afford to forget that instructors are students as well. Instructor evaluations will identify opportunities to improve. Training managers should plan instructor development activities on at least a quarterly basis.

Instructor development activities can include:

- Conference calls to discuss a concern and brainstorm about ways to address that area;
- Sending out a reprint of a relevant article;
- Conduct a webinar to showcase a particularly good instructor or session;
- Have a formal training session.

Each training manager should set up development activities that promote self-awareness of abilities and a culture of improvement, rather than a punitive environment.

## Instructor Importance

Deciding what qualifies an individual as an instructor for a specific course or class is very different from selecting the right instructor for a class. Program managers must maintain an accurate inventory of each instructor's tool set so that assignments are made in the best interests of the training organization and students.

The process of identifying and vetting instructors for an organization or program is time-consuming and detail-oriented. However, the training organization has an ethical responsibility to provide qualified, capable instructors for programs they offer. Instructors are the ones directly responsible for bridging between the curricula, the technology, the environment and students. Instructors define students, which in turn define the training organization.

# APPENDIX A: THE LEARNING MANAGEMENT SYSTEM

## What is an LMS?

A Learning Management System (or LMS) is a software package, usually on a large scale (that scale is decreasing rapidly), that enables the management and delivery of learning content and resources to students. Most LMS systems are web-based to facilitate "anytime, anywhere" access to learning content and administration.

At a minimum, the LMS usually allows for student registration, the delivery and tracking of e-learning courses and content, and testing, and may also allow for the management of instructor-led training classes. In the most comprehensive of LMSs, one may find tools such as competency management, skills-gap analysis, succession planning, certifications, virtual live classes, and resource allocation (venues, rooms, textbooks, instructors, etc.). Most systems allow for learner self-service, facilitating self-enrollment, and access to courses.

Some LMS vendors do not distinguish between LMS and LCMS, preferring to refer to both under the term "LMS", but there is a difference. The LCMS, which stands for "Learning Content Management System", facilitates organization of content from authoring tools, and presentation of this content to students via the LMS.

LMSs are based on a variety of development platforms, from Java EE based architectures to Microsoft .NET, and usually employ the use of a robust database back-end. While most systems are commercially developed, free and open-source models do exist. Other than the most simplistic, basic functionality, all LMSs cater to, and focus on different educational, administrative, and deployment requirements.

## Do You Need a LMS? The 3-Question Test

What defines the need for a learning management system? A learning management system is an investment that should produce a measurable return and become an integral part of the overall learning strategy. There are some pretty common reasons training managers begin an initial search into learning management systems:

- Managing a department responsible for training others or monitoring job skills
- Frustration with spreadsheets and databases currently in use
- Creating individual e-mails to students, instructors, etc.
- Using HTML or PDF forms to register students for training
- Grading exams manually
- Printing and mailing student certificates

- Charging fees for training or materials

When investigating the need for a learning management system, there are three basic questions to ask.

## 1. Do I spend a lot of time on tasks that could be automated?

Automation of daily tasks in the training center can not only save time, it can help the center grow without additional staff. Automated confirmation letters and reminder notices helps to increase attendance rates. Automating student history requests and certificate delivery reduces the amount of staff time spent handling calls and e-mails. With a LMS, a job title or membership in department or assigned group can automate assignment to training. Instructors can be notified via e-mail when they are assigned to teach a specific class. Automation of day-to-day tasks is a major benefit of a learning management system.

### Student Registration

Each training center has unique methods – traditional classroom sessions, self-paced online programs, or even webinars. With a learning management system, students can easily register for being offered. Learning management systems allow the training manager to control minimum and maximum registrations for specific programs. Most offer the ability to create multi-step registration approval processes. Multi-step approvals ensure that all the affected parties are aware of a student's request – for example, if the student's registration could result in overtime. Training managers can also usually control wait-listing.

### Communication

Communication is key in any training organization. Students expect to receive training announcements, registration confirmations, and alerts for any change in a class location or schedule. Clear, effective communication ensures students arrive prepared for class. Confirmation letters can include directions to the site, instructor contact information, and almost any other information the training manager wishes to provide. Send a quick thank you note to all attendees automatically the day after class concludes. Follow-up e-mails can also be used to clear up the issue or provide links to additional information.

### Confirmation

When students register for a class but subsequently fail to attend training it affects the organization. A learning management system can be configured to send reminder e-mails to students asking them to confirm their attendance or cancel the registration. Confirmation e-mails can include specific directions to a room or site and instructor contact information. Last minute changes to a class can be easily integrated to the confirmation e-mail. For self-paced learning activities, the confirmation can include the pertinent links or access information.

*Marketing*

An LMS allows the training center to communicate information on new training program or services that students may be interested in. With automated communications, a training center can easily reach out to students who need refresher or recertification training. Automatically generate marketing e-mails based on demographics, classes taken or not taken, or group assignments within the learning management system.

## 2. Do I need to centralize, secure and share data?

A learning management system is a window into the activity of a training center. Data can be used to show training's support of business goals. A learning management system creates a central repository for training data. Rather than information being locked away in an office filing cabinet, a learning management system allows authorized individuals to access information at any time.

*Centralization*

Data centralization is a key benefit of a learning management system. Permissions allow an authorized user access to data and tasks relevant to their role in the training center. Students want to know what classes are still accepting, instructors want to know who has registered for their class, and staff members want to know the status of the training center at any given time. Centralized data provides real-time data access, helping all users make better decisions with up-to-date information. Centralized data also helps ensure data security and reliability. Data centralization allows for easy backup and storage for business continuity purposes. Convert older paper records into a standard document type such as Adobe PDF™ and attach them to the appropriate record in the learning management system.

*Sharing Data*

A learning management system allows users to rapidly create and share meaningful reports. A training manager must be able to readily explain how efficiently training is being delivered, and how effective that training is. A good learning management system provides both big picture operating statistics and granular metrics to help analyze the true health of training.

Occasions will arise where a training manager will have to work with large amounts of data. Whether adding 150 employees from a newly acquired company as students, or exporting information to the company's enterprise accounting system, a learning management system should easily move data.

## 3. Do I need to deliver programs, courses or classes online?

Self-paced instructional activity (distributed learning, e-learning, etc.) is a third major reason to consider use of a learning management system. A learning management system can facilitate a variety of learning activities, including:

- Fully interactive classes, such as SCORM-conformant material produced using Adobe's Captivate, Articulate's Engage, or Techsmith's Camtasia software.

- Launched classes, where the content is developed and/or hosted at another location.
- Other self-paced classes, such as computer-based or video-based training and webinars.

Simply, a learning management system should allow a training center to deliver the content to students in the most appropriate method.

### Learning Management Systems: The Next Step

Answering "yes" to any one of these questions is sufficient reason to consider a learning management system. These systems are an investment that can provide a training center a solid return on investment and multiply the efforts of a small training department.

## Things an LMS Doesn't Do

Before rushing to speak to vendors, training managers should also understand that a learning management system is a tool. A hammer is of very limited use when changing a tire, and a learning management system has limitations as well. Although there are hundreds of articles discussing opinions on what constitutes a "good" system there are far fewer articles that explain what a learning management system will not do.

A Learning Management System:

### ...Doesn't Create Content

Curt Bonk postulated that "most course management systems fail to provide creative sparks to learning because they only track or map it after it occurs." Well, in one sense he's right – systems do fail because of the content. But there is not a single system on the market that uses artificial intelligence (AI) to create training content. So, the course management system is not what fails to provide the spark – the content itself fails. A learning management system promotes access to content, facilitates delivery of content, tracks interaction with content, and assists the training manager In evaluating outcomes.

The responsibility for creating an educational spark lies with the individuals creating the content within the learning management system. Well-created content is time-consuming and difficult to produce, and should be tracking and mapping interaction throughout delivery. That's part of the reason the SCORM standards exist. A good learning management system is a tool for the content creation team, not a replacement for it. A learning management system should support delivery of content in whatever manner best supports the educational need.

Beware of systems that restrict training to specific forms of content – SCORM, AICC, PDF, video, etc. A learning management system is a framework for content delivery and use. Avoid handcuffing the instructional design team to a singular format, development tool or standard.

### ...Doesn't Ensure Training Success

More than one training center has invested heavily in a learning management system, only to continue struggling with training and development issues. Purchasing or replacing a learning management system is not a "magic bullet" and does not guarantee success. Purchasing an expensive lawn mower doesn't guarantee a beautiful yard. The training center must spend time creating content of interest and value, then market that content to the stakeholders. A good learning management system should have excellent marketing and branding tools even if all the training is conducted for free.

Issues rarely addressed by learning management system companies and increasingly forgotten by training centers are "low tech" and "no tech" users. A web-based LMS does nothing for the individual that doesn't have internet access. The needs of those users are equally important. A learning management system will not be successful if it fails to track traditional (classroom) or on-the-job (skills-based) learning. Likewise, instructional designers may have to create variations of content and content delivery mechanisms to reach these users.

### ...Won't Replace Instructors

One of the basic functions of a learning management system is to deliver content. A LMS has the advantage of delivering content at any time, consistently. In that respect a LMS does replace one of the instructor's duties. However, a learning management system does not respond to student questions, moderate discussions, interact with students via social media, or return voice mail messages. A learning management system may grade some types of assignments or exams, but cannot assign grades to discussion board posts or research papers. Instructors are still needed because a learning management system cannot visit a work site and provide corrective feedback or conduct a learning lab skills session. A LMS should be able to capture the instructor's observation of these activities.

### ...Doesn't Run Itself

Purchase of a learning management system doesn't replace the individuals with responsibility for training. Just like other tools, the learning management system requires maintenance and attention to detail. There will always be maintenance operations – updating class schedules, assisting students with their accounts, merging duplicate accounts, et cetera. A learning management system automates many functions and multiplies what a training staff can accomplish. An LMS cannot simply be purchased, installed, and forgotten.

Understanding what an LMS will not do for a training center is an important step. Certainly, a well-configured and maintained learning management system can yield an excellent return on investment and be an excellent addition to corporate training.

## Three Reasons to Change Learning Management Systems

Learning management systems are major investments. There are numerous studies and reports floating around that support the notion that many LMS customers are unhappy.

One survey by the eLearning Guild places the number of customers planning to change vendors as high as 13%. That may be true, but in today's economy the cost of changing vendors cannot be justified by subjective opinions. Many training managers have spent hours researching change, talking with vendors and preparing proposals, only to be shot down by a board of directors or senior manager.

So when is it appropriate to change to a new learning management system vendor? Rarely is a single factor adequate; usually it is a combination of cost, technology, and vendor concerns. Examining and proposing a change must focus on the objective business circumstances, not a subjective opinion. Consider how the change can generate:

- Wage, labor, and personnel cost savings, including reduced turnover
- Increased productivity or decreased cost per training unit
- Revenue from expansion of training
- Miscellaneous returns, such as decreased maintenance costs or improved sales tactics

Carefully consider how such a change will affect the training staff, as well. Consider the personal fatigue and delay on during the transition. As part of the training team, training managers will be responsible for most of the change process.

## 1. Cost

As the number of learning management system vendors have increased, so have the variety of price points and options. Cost is a common component of most change proposals. A learning management system that is priced based on computers, students, or class volume can get very expensive if a training center experiences rapid success and growth. Other vendors have placed fees on things like data storage or bandwidth usage to increase revenue. Ideally, training centers should be able to budget a specific annual amount to cover their learning management system needs.

There are number of factors to consider when considering a switch based on cost. When presenting a proposal, include these items in the cost analysis. Be clear that the cost savings are worth the effort involved in the switch.

### Features

"Never build your feature list in a vendor hall" is great advice. If cost is a primary motive for a change, adding new features can negate the cost savings. Make a list of the features that are used on a daily basis by the training center staff, instructors, students and other users.

### Cost of Transition

In addition to the quoted price from potential vendors, there will be a significant amount of time and effort involved in any transition. How is existing data going to be supplied by the current provider?  Some vendors store information in a proprietary manner, and charge fees for extracting data to a usable format.  How much work is involved to import the data and set up the new system?  What amount of time will be required from the information technology department to implement the change?  How long will the system be off-line, and are there any business processes affected?  How much time will be required to train personnel on use of the new system?  The costs associated with a transition can rapidly eliminate potential savings.

*Long-Term Costs*

After looking at the cost of transition, return to daily business processes and evaluate both learning management systems' feature set.  What tasks will change?  How will changes affect training center staff?  Does cutting cost and features mean the training center staff will have less time to teach? Less time to develop new material?

## 2. Technology

Technology changes at a very rapid rate. Education and training web sites are filled with press releases, advertisements and editorials on new approaches and features.  Avoid the technical imperative – creating a need for a feature just because the feature exists. Consider technology as it relates specifically to the training center, students and curricula.

- Technology that decreases the cost of training delivery, compared to the existing learning management system.
- The need to integrate with technologies or systems being adopted by the company on a larger scale.
- Transitioning from a self-hosted solution to a vendor-hosted (cloud, SaaS) solution.
- Technology that relates to ease-of-use, accessibility, or increased automation.
- Technology that increases transfer of training to the work environment.
- Significant growth that challenges the capabilities of the existing learning management system (server load, simultaneous users, bandwidth, capacity, etc.)

When proposing a switch based on changes in technology, remember to address the cost issue.  Show how the change in technology will have a significant return on investment over time.  Also, show how continuing with the current learning management system will begin to negatively impact the training center and company.

## 3. Vendor

Dissatisfaction with a vendor often comes when expectations and responsibilities are not clearly defined or understood. Some of the most common vendor issues cited in change proposals are:

- Dissatisfaction with impersonal support and support responsiveness

- Addition of "hidden" costs throughout the contract life
- "Down" time or problems maintaining an acceptable service level
- Lack of a voice in future development and not anticipating needs
- Failure to provide software updates or patches
- Unresponsive to customization, personalization, or reporting requests

Citing issues with the learning management system vendor as the reason for a switch is potentially the most difficult to justify. The corporate management team will have questions that a training manager should be prepared to answer:

- "Are these issues covered by existing written agreements or documents?"
- "Has the vendor's management team been contacted and the issue(s) clearly voiced the issue?"
- "How did the vendor respond?"
- "If the issue remains unresolved, what is the impact to our business?"

Be prepared for the management team to suggest reaching back out to the current vendor and working with them to find solutions. A training manager may have to approach the management team several times, updating the change proposal with additional information. If possible, place a financial amount on how much the unresolved vendor issue has "cost" between each approach.

### Your New Learning Management System Vendor

When proposing a switch, remember to be open and honest with the newly selected vendor. Be sure to understand key differences between systems. If vendor issues are an element of the decision, be sure expectations are clearly outlined and understood by both parties. Develop a successful implementation plan.

The decision to implement or change learning management systems is rarely a quick decision. Be sure any actions are based on a solid, objective business case. Clearly articulate how the change will have a positive impact.

## Selecting a Learning Management System

With the large number of vendors offering training or learning management software, making a purchase decision is tougher than ever.

Selecting a system to manage training data is a complex process, and there are a huge number of factors to consider. Satisfaction with a single system or vendor is often determined by conversations and discussions that occur months before a purchase order is signed or a check written. The most satisfied customers usually have a clear understanding of what a system is expected to do and how that system integrates into the overall learning strategy and business model.

Although every training organization is unique, there are some basic steps to help ensure the proper system gets put in place. Before any selection process begins, gather a group of stakeholders - staff members, instructors, and students. Involve these stakeholders throughout the process.

### Understand the Learning Strategy

A learning management system should be a good bridge between the overall business model and delivery of training content. The learning strategy should define how educational programs are delivered to the right people to meet specific business goals.

As a learning organization, there should already be a clearly defined strategy in place. As the LMS selection process begins, the time is right to review and clarify the strategy. The learning strategy should always reflect the target audience, their learning preferences, their locations, the resources that are available to them to attend learning programs, et cetera.

Correlate the strategy with the company's business goals. Many companies have mission or vision statements, corporate values, and strategic plans. A training manager should be able to clearly articulate how training aligns to these higher-level elements.

### Document Your Needs

Once the strategy is defined, identify what resources and technologies are needed to implement the strategy. Compile these requirements into a single document, called an LMS specifications document. This internal requirements document is not the same as a request for proposal (RFP). The specifications document becomes a tool from which an RFP is generated.

Use care when writing out needs. Buzzwords and vendor-specific features can be very distracting. The specifications document should be created before speaking with a vendor or doing any research; the focus should be entirely on defining the training center's actual need. Avoid specifying requirements that fail to contribute to the learning strategy or business model.

The more thoroughly specifications are crafted, the more accurate the resulting RFP will be. For example, a need statement might be "Web pages must follow corporate style guidelines." This need turns into a number of line items within the RFP for editing pages, inserting logos, and creating themes. The resulting RFP requirements could include applying logos to printed documents or setting the format for outgoing e-mails.

One of the most common mistakes training managers make on RFP's is to use overly-generalized requirements. While the statement "customizable reports" is an appropriate element of a specification, if the same statement was used in an RFP the door is opened to misinterpretation. The vendor may believe the customer wants to filter or sort data; the customer actually wanted to apply the company logo to the printed report.

*Hosted Services: ASP's, SaaS, and the Cloud*

One of the first major decisions to be made in the selection process is whether the system will be hosted by the company or the vendor. Although there are many names for this type of hosted service, the basic concept has existed since the late 1990's. Application Service Providers (ASP's) provide software applications to users remotely using a network, usually the Internet.

Many of today's applications are provided solely over the Internet. As network bandwidth has increased in homes and businesses, a larger number of software products are available only as browser-based applications. Recently, the terms Software-as-a-Service (SaaS) and "cloud" computing have become popular. Both are essentially an extension of the original ASP concept. Many early ASP's required the installation of software on a user's computer. Today's hosted solutions require very little from the client's computer. Installation consists of accessing the site, and possibly the installation of a browser plug-in.

There are several advantages to a vendor-hosted system:

- No software has to be installed or maintained locally,
- Application patches, fixes and updates can be easily applied,
- Hosted solutions are generally less expensive,
- Vendors tend to update applications more frequently, and
- Customizations can be made more quickly and inexpensively.

Many training managers and organizations select a hosted solution because the vendor absorbs the cost associated with maintaining a complex information technology infrastructure. The costs of installing and maintaining a dedicated server are significant. A hosted solution also minimizes the impact on information technology personnel. Information technology personnel should help develop requirements and service level agreements.

When writing requirements related to hosting, consider the following:

- Avoid specifying "uptime" values, especially ones that are unrealistic (i.e., 100%). With many of today's hosting providers, the value of requiring "uptime" is greatly diminished. Instead, consider specifying response times for customer support.
- Define low-traffic windows when the vendor can perform server maintenance, patches, and upgrades. Having these windows defined ensures that down time can be communicated to users and minimize impact on the training center.
- The nature and types of support that are necessary,
- A list of concerns or issues and an expected resolution time frame,

- Minimum/maximum contract length and extension process, and
- Ownership and structure of data, including backups and business continuity processes.

## Cost, Needs, and Wants

Although early in the process, a training manager must begin balancing costs against critical needs, general needs, and wants. A top-of-the-line learning management system fully customized by the vendor, can easily cost a company $100,000 or more annually. Eliminating a few features and taking on the task of customizing the system using the vendor's tool set can significantly reduce cost, but requires staff time.

Prioritize requirements based on whether an item is mission-critical or simply "nice to have". Use a ranking scale to prioritize. The advisory or peer review groups can be of some assistance. Once the requirements are identified, share the list and ask the group to assign priorities based on each member's views and needs. Add group feedback into the specifications document.

## Developing the LMS Specification

The following tables identify a number of common LMS features. Many vendors provide similar information, but are often designed to steer a training organization towards that vendor. Use caution when using vendor-supplied tools to evaluate or compare learning management systems.

## Sample LMS Specification

This table is available as a Microsoft Excel document from the Oak Tree Systems' site: https://www.dropbox.com/sh/z19kxslkjo3hvlg/yzbzGYAycu .

| | | | Use this block to help identify and quantify needs. Use letters (C-Critical, N-Nice to Have, etc.) to identify features beneficial to the training center. |
|---|---|---|---|
| | ↓ | ↓ | Once all needed features have been identified, use the secondary block to prioritize the need. |
| Ex | C | 7 | *All access to the LMS occurs via web browser.* |
| **USER ACCESS** | | | |
| 1. | | | All access to the LMS occurs via web browser. |
| 2. | | | Allows multiple, fully customizable portals. |
| 3. | | | Allows for single sign-on using established credentials. |
| 4. | | | User-level password management tools, controlled by System Administrator. |
| 5. | | | Allows students, instructors, and training coordinators to retrieve or reset passwords based on site settings. |
| **DATA MANAGEMENT & REPORTING** | | | |
| 6. | | | No restrictions on bandwidth. |
| 7. | | | No restrictions on database size. |
| 8. | | | Database backup copies readily available via web interface. |
| 9. | | | Data segregation allowed by user-defined regions |
| 10. | | | Regions may be associated with a specific portal |

| | | | |
|---|---|---|---|
| 11. | | | Restrict access to data / tools based on group membership. |
| 12. | | | Advanced import of existing training data. |
| 13. | | | Allows creation of custom user fields. |
| 14. | | | Allows creation of custom user fields for courses, classes, instructors, organizations, and students. |
| 15. | | | Allows the upload of files to courses, organizations, or students. |
| 16. | | | Allows for a default time zone. |
| 17. | | | The local time zone can be specified for each training activity (especially important for automated communications and appointment reminders). |
| 18. | | | Maintains a configurable audit trail. |
| **COURSE / CLASS MANAGEMENT** | | | |
| 19. | | | Allows for rapid creation of courses. |
| 20. | | | Allows for creation of multiple classes for a single course. |
| 21. | | | Classes for a course can include multiple delivery methods (self-paced, classroom, webinar). |
| 22. | | | Allows specific courses to be packaged together as part of an educational program. |
| 23. | | | Allows for direct linking / launching of external content for a specific class. |
| 24. | | | Allows multiple-session class schedules (including non-contiguous days). |
| 25. | | | Allows the creation of schedule templates for rapid entry of similar sessions. |
| 26. | | | Allows establishing minimum and maximum student counts, including a maximum registration count for self-paced classes. *(Wait-listing supported, see* Registration) |
| 27. | | | Allows training activity to be set to an Inactive status without deletion of content or records. |
| 28. | | | Allows SCORM ☐ 3rd Edition ☐ 4th Edition Content |
| 29. | | | Allows AICC Content |
| 30. | | | Allows for the printing of student name badges. |
| 31. | | | Class certificates are fully customizable for each course. |
| 32. | | | Allows users to print certificates for successfully completed learning activities directly from the internet browser. |
| 33. | | | Class confirmation letters are fully customizable.. |
| 34. | | | Includes an internal notes field for classes and courses, accessible only to training staff members. |
| 35. | | | Allows users to make course and class requests. |
| 36. | | | Student attendance data tracked by class meeting. |
| 37. | | | Attaches calendar appointments (.ics files) to training activities. |
| 38. | | | Allows training staff to add, update, reschedule, and remove courses and content quickly and intuitively. |
| 39. | | | Allows access to registration, attendance, completion and grades for all courses. |
| 40. | | | Allows assignment of materials (books, etc.) to training activity as course materials, for sale items, or both. |
| 41. | | | Allows materials assigned to courses to be used on a set quantity per instructor, per registrant, or per class basis. |

| | | |
|---|---|---|
| 42. | | Class status easily identified (accepting, full, started, cancelled, ended, and completed). |
| 43. | | Allows for specification of pre-requisites. |
| **STUDENT MANAGEMENT** | | |
| 44. | | Students can manage/update their personal information. |
| 45. | | Allows for student self-service account creation. |
| 46. | | Allows multiple methods for administrative creation of students. |
| 47. | | Allows rapid import of students via an Excel spreadsheet. |
| 48. | | Training staff can rapidly merge multiple student records, in the event of duplicate account creation. |
| 49. | | Allows for use of an Alternate ID as part of the student's profile (badge number, employee identification number, credential number, etc.). |
| 50. | | Allows use of the Alternate ID as a method of log in to the portal. |
| 51. | | Allows students to be assigned as a manager or to a manager. |
| 52. | | Allows students to be assigned as a mentor or to a mentor. |
| 53. | | Allows students to be assigned to multiple groups simultaneously. |
| 54. | | Allows students to be assigned to a specific job title and inherit associated skills / competency requirements. |
| 55. | | Allows students to be assigned to a specific training plan. |
| 56. | | Includes an internal notes field for each student. |
| **INSTRUCTOR TOOLS / MANAGEMENT** | | |
| 57. | | Allows instructors to post attendance, completion, and grade information via their portal. |
| 58. | | Allows assignment of instructors as qualified to teach specific courses. |
| 59. | | Allows instructors to view their teaching schedule via the web portal |
| 60. | | Allows instructors to view registrations for their class via the web portal |
| 61. | | Allows instructors to approve/decline registrations (if an approval process is used) via the web portal |
| 62. | | Allows instructors to print student sign-in sheets directly from the web portal. |
| 63. | | Allows multiple instructor roles when assigned to a training session. |
| 64. | | Allows instructors to document student skill demonstration or observation directly from the web portal. |
| **REGISTRATION / REGISTRAR FUNCTIONS** | | |
| 65. | | Web-based self-service registration for all portal users, for all training types (classroom and self-paced learning) |
| 66. | | Scheduled classes can include classroom, classroom with remote attendees, and webinars. |
| 67. | | Self-Paced classes can include online, video, CBT, self-study opportunities. |
| 68. | | Immediate e-mail confirmation of student registration (or registration request if approval is required). |
| 69. | | Allows a registration approval process, where a potential student's registration must be approved or declined by a specific role or individual. |
| 70. | | Creation of course-specific, fully customizable class rosters (sign-in sheets). |
| 71. | | Automatic creation and display of course / class calendar. |

| 72. | | | Class enrollment information readily visible to instructional staff, including class status and student count (registered, maximum seats, waiting). |
|---|---|---|---|
| 73. | | | Class details available including availability, schedule, location(s), prerequisites, summary, agenda and pricing. |
| 74. | | | Allows instructional staff to set a cancellation cut-off date at the class level. |
| 75. | | | Allows self-service cancellation for portal users prior to cancellation cut-off date, or 30 days after the start of a self-paced class. |
| 76. | | | Allows enforcement of prerequisites prior to registration. |
| 77. | | | Allows overrides to prerequisites by training center staff. |
| 78. | | | Waiting list behavior customizable by training center staff. |
| 79. | | | Allows overrides to the waiting list by training center staff. |
| 80. | | | Allows overrides to maximum enrollment by training center staff. |
| 81. | | | Allows specified users to register students within their organization(s). |
| 82. | | | Allows training center staff to register students. |
| 83. | | | Allows each user access to a complete training history/transcript. |
| 84. | | | Supports manual entry of external training history by training center staff. |
| **LOCATION / RESOURCE MANAGEMENT** | | | |
| 85. | | | Supports training locations as a separate entity from organizations. |
| 86. | | | Allows entry of directions, map URL, nearby hotels and airports for each location. |
| 87. | | | Allows multiple rooms per location, with capacity information. |
| 88. | | | Allows room reservation / scheduling, including details on "closed" dates and pricing. |
| 89. | | | Allows for detailed information on educational resources, including purchase and vendor information and pricing. |
| 90. | | | Allows for assignment or reservation of resource slots to students. *Resource slots allow assignment of a student to particular resource through the use of time slots.* |
| 91. | | | Identifies and supports resolution of location, room, instructor, or resource conflicts |
| 92. | | | Allows for restriction of locations, rooms, and resources based on group membership. |
| 93. | | | Automatic creation and display of location and resource calendar(s). |
| 94. | | | Reports on resource utilization. |
| **ASSESSMENT TOOLS (EXAMS & SURVEYS)** | | | |
| 95. | | | Allow assignment of pre-class surveys or examinations |
| 96. | | | Allow creation of surveys and exams consisting of common question types. |
| 97. | | | Allows the use of external content (PDF, video, audio) in support of questions for surveys and exams. |
| 98. | | | Allows assignment of individual question item weights, passing score, and completion time limits. |
| 99. | | | Allows analysis of student survey and exam responses by question and by comparison between postings. |

| 100. | | Allow exporting of raw response information from surveys and exams to multiple formats. |
|---|---|---|
| 101. | | Allow rapid creation of surveys and exams by cloning previously created postings. |
| 102. | | Allow student review of answer(s). |
| 103. | | Completion of a survey or exam affects the student's history as selected by training center staff: completing item completes class; completing item with a passing score completes the class; or does not affect class completion. |
| 104. | | Allows survey responses to be recorded anonymously. |
| 105. | | Surveys and examinations are available only within a date range specified by the training center staff. |
| **FINANCIAL / ACCOUNTING** | | |
| 106. | | Allows training center staff to set an accounting status (good standing, past due, probation, suspended) for student and organization. |
| 107. | | Payment options controlled by accounting status. |
| 108. | | Supports invoicing and aging of accounts. |
| 109. | | Allows Invoices to be imported from within QuickBooks, or exported to legacy systems. |
| 110. | | Allows combining of invoices for each organization. |
| 111. | | Supports complex pricing models, including quantity matrices. |
| 112. | | Supports the sale and use of vouchers, payment plans, contracts, master purchase orders, and passive billing. |
| 113. | | Supports the sale of materials through portal pages. |
| 114. | | Supports merchant credit card processing. |
| 115. | | Supports "no charge" pricing. |
| **MARKETING** | | |
| 116. | | Allows marketing communication based on region, profile filters, and class taken/not taken filters, among others. |
| **REPORTING** | | |
| 117. | | Extensive report generators with common reports, with intuitive filtering of data. |
| 118. | | Allows creation of reports in multiple formats, including Adobe PDF, Microsoft Excel, Comma Separated Value (CSV), and HTML. |
| 119. | | Training Metrics summary reports. |
| 120. | | Skill / Competency summary reports. |
| 121. | | Ability to modify and save reports for re-use. |
| 122. | | Ability to export raw data for analysis. |
| 123. | | Allows creation of custom reports using existing data sources. |
| **USER CUSTOMIZATION CAPABILITY** | | |
| 124. | | Student portal page(s) are fully editable / customizable using HTML. |
| 125. | | Portal headers/footers, instructions, and help editable. |
| 126. | | Pre-defined, user-selectable themes for portals. |
| 127. | | Visual data representation using pre-defined charts and graphs. |
| 128. | | Charts and graphs can be saved for use in management presentations. |
| 129. | | Document templates are fully editable, including merge fields. |
| **AUTOMATED EVENT MANAGEMENT / AUTOMATED COMMUNICATIONS** | | |
| 130. | | Allows automated e-mail generation for specific events. |

| | | | |
|---|---|---|---|
| 131. | | | Allows customization of e-mail documents for use by automated events. |
| 132. | | | Allows creation of and editing of automated events. |
| 133. | | | Allows students to post reviews of a course or class. |
| 134. | | | Maintains document templates for automated communications, with easy insertion of database merge fields based on the template type. |
| 135. | | | Maintains a communications log for each student, including date, time and the merged document. |
| 136. | | | Marketing Wizard allows Staff Members to rapidly e-mail a document template or export a set of student records based on rules set in the wizard. |
| 137. | | | Does the Event Manager allow for specific events to be written to a log file instead of e-mailing a specific document? ☐ Yes ☐ No |
| 138. | | | Does the event manager allow Staff Members to assign the recipient of the automated communication? ☐ Yes ☐ No |
| 139. | | | Does the event management tool allow Staff Members to copy other parties based on their role (i.e., student's manager, student's mentor, organization training coordinator, etc.)? ☐ Yes ☐ No |
| 140. | | | Does the event management tool allow selection of the originator (sender) of the automated e-mail? ☐ Yes ☐ No |
| 141. | | | Of registration (registration confirmation). |
| 142. | | | Of instructor assignment to teach a course. |
| 143. | | | Of course / class scheduling or availability. |
| 144. | | | Automated follow-up reminders for upcoming scheduled classes. |
| 145. | | | When a date, time, or facility changes. |
| 146. | | | When a class reaches the maximum enrollment. |
| 147. | | | When a course or class request is received. |
| 148. | | | When course or class is created. |
| 149. | | | When a class is available for registration. |
| 150. | | | When database records are deleted. |
| 151. | | | Of registration cancellations. |
| 152. | | | Approving party notified of a registration request. |
| 153. | | | Of an approving party's decision regarding a registration request. |
| 154. | | | When a selfpaced class Is passed. |
| 155. | | | When an exam is completed – passed. |
| 156. | | | When an exam is completed – failed. |
| 157. | | | When a survey is completed. |
| 158. | | | When a resource assigned to a class is changed. |
| 159. | | | When a skill or competency is past due. |
| 160. | | | When a skill is obtained. |
| **SUPPORT & SOFTWARE UPDATES** | | | |
| 161. | | | Software updates, patches, and fixes included in the price (including major upgrades) for the subscription period. |
| 162. | | | Online support portal to interface with vendor. |
| 163. | | | Telephone and e-mail support included in the subscription cost. |
| 164. | | | Support is done internally by the vendor staff. |
| **SKILL & COMPETENCY MANAGEMENT** | | | |

| 165. | | | Assignment of skills/competencies and packages to job titles, students, or equipment |
|------|--|--|----------------------------------------------------------------------------------------|
| 166. | | | Allows acquisition of a skill or competency through completion of a specific course, by demonstration, or by observation. |
| 167. | | | Allows for each acquired skill or competency to have a specific life span (expiration). |
| 168. | | | Allows bundling of skills or competency into skills packages. |
| 169. | | | Skills packages can be assigned by job title or equipment. |
| 170. | | | Track and report on learner/organization activity and progress by skills / competency; including knowledge gaps based on assigned Training Plans. |

## Create and Validate the Budget

The training manager should establish a specific budget for the purchase. The price range for a learning management system varies widely. Simple, low-usage systems can be found for under $10,000 per year. Complex, customized systems can carry a price tag of $250,000 per year or more. There are some basic line items that should be included in the budget:

### Preparation & Research Expenses

Time and expenses associated with research, preparing the requirements, issuing a Request for Proposal, evaluating proposals and conducting subsequent meetings, and negotiating the final agreement with the selected vendor. Although these may be a part of the training manager's job description, these tasks represent an expense associated with the purchase. Keep track of time spent and the resulting expense.

### Purchase of a Solution

The purchase price of the software or subscription.

### Customization

Allow an amount for customizations. Very few solutions are a perfect fit upon implementation. Each vendor has rates and methods for pricing customizations. Including 10% of the purchase price for customization as a separate line item provides a lot of flexibility once the solution is in place.

### Data Migration / Conversion

If transitioning from an existing system or planning to import paper or spreadsheet-based data into the system, include a line item covering data conversion. Many vendors include simple conversion as part of their service. Other vendors may provide tools within the software product which allow the training center to import data. Almost all vendors will migrate or convert data for a fee. Because a vendor is experienced with manipulating raw data, often it can be both cheaper and more efficient to include data migration in the budget even if do-it-yourself tools exist .

<u>Training</u>

Training stakeholders on the implementation of a new system is one of the most overlooked costs. Almost every vendor will send a trainer or specialist to a new customer's site early in the implementation process to both train personnel and assist with implementation. Unfortunately, many training managers insist "training isn't needed" and eliminate vendor-provided training from any quotation and purchase.

---

**Not purchasing vendor-provided training in a learning management system purchase is the single most expensive mistake a training manager can make.**

---

On-site training is expensive, but the gain in productivity and decrease in the staff's learning curve far outweighs the cost of training. Assume a vendor charges $5,000 for on-site training and provides a support webinars for larger distribution. If training reduces the amount of time for training staff to get "up and running" by as little as 25%, productivity gains far exceed the cost of training in just the first year. The vendor also gains insight into the company's business model and can be a much better partner over the long term.

<u>Support & Maintenance</u>

Ensure a specific amount for support and maintenance is included in the budget. If hosting the solution on company servers (self-hosting), be sure to include any future hardware or software upgrades that may be necessary in the budget. Estimate the labor costs of the internal information technology department to maintain the installation.

Vendor-hosted solutions often include support and maintenance costs as part of the subscription. The vendor benefits from having all customers use the same product version, rather than trying to support multiple products.

Once a budget is established, share it with other decision-makers in the training center.

## RESEARCH POTENTIAL VENDORS

After defining needs and preparing the budget, begin to research potential vendors. Identify vendors that provide specific features designated a high priority. Look at non-sponsored research in addition to research on the web. Use multiple keywords when searching; there are a large number of vendors (over 500, as of July 2012) that provide learning management systems. Identify business criteria that are important. Consider:

- What is the vendor's company status - is ownership stable?
- Is the company privately or publicly held? Review annual reports of public companies.
- How long has the vendor been in business overall?
- How long has the vendor been in the training or learning management market?
- Does the vendor use 3rd-Party product components in the product offering?

- Does the vendor hire and retain their product development personnel, or outsource/contract development?

Match all vendor features to the needs document. Create a simple spreadsheet with needs listed in rows, and potential vendors as columns. Group features by priority in rows. Use the vendor's web site, product documentation, product videos, etc. to determine whether a feature is present. Use research time wisely – if a vendor cannot meet critical requirements, spend less time researching them.

Also remember that the purchase decision is not based on this research – this part of the process is just to identify companies best positioned to submit a proposal. Create a reasonable list of firms from which proposals will be sought. Be sure to consider at least one firm from within the same locality, state or region if at all possible.

### Prepare a Request for Proposal (RFP)

Writing a Request for Proposal (RFP) or other type of quote document can be challenging. Many vendors offer specifications criteria or sample RFP documents. Use these resources wisely. The needs document and initial research will be combined as the RFP is crafted.

An RFP accurately reflects a training center's needs in the following areas:

- Business needs (pricing, length of term, etc.)
- Technical / infrastructure requirements
- Product requirements
- Implementation timetable and performance benchmarks

Training managers occasionally have a purchasing department or procurement specialist available for assistance. There are many resources on the web to help create an RFP. When writing individual requirements, be specific. The items should require a vendor to respond in detail, not simply by checking a box.

Which RFP item provides the training manager useful information?

| RFP Example Item 1 | |
|---|---|
| 231 | Registration document templates must be customizable. |  ☐ Y  ☐ N |

| RFP Example Item 2 | |
|---|---|
| 231 | Registration document templates must be customizable.  Describe how the LMS allows users to customize registration templates / documents. |
| | |

RFPs serve two purposes. First, the vendors' RFP responses allow a more detailed comparison of products without being distracted by promotional literature or hype.

Second, once a vendor is selected, the vendor's statements in the RFP help form the training manager's expectations as a customer.

Scenarios are a normal part of many training programs. Include scenario-based questions as part of the RFP so the vendor can clearly explain how that scenario will be handled by the product.

The time from issuance of the RFP until vendor proposals must be in hand should be short but reasonable. Most vendors can respond to an RFP within a two-week time frame. A short response time also gives the training center an indication of how hard a company will work for the business. How a vendor responds to an RFP request can also be an indicator as to how the vendor will perform in a business relationship.

The vendor should include a proposed project plan for implementation based on the requirements as part of the RFP submission. The plan must include timelines relative to the start and end of the project, providing an estimate as to how long the vendor believes an implementation will take. The plan should also specify ownership and details for each task or step in the implementation process. Most vendors have a "road map" for implementation that can be easily adapted and included with proposals.

A final note about RFPs – show courtesy to the vendor, as well. Some RFPs for multi-year, multi-million dollar contracts can number into the hundreds of pages. Most vendors invest significant time and expense in preparing RFP responses. Only submit RFP's to vendors that have a realistic chance of winning the training center's business. Be sure the RFP is as complete as necessary, while keeping it simple. The RFP should also include an overview of the budget available for the project; doing so shows the vendor the training center is committed to implementing a solution. Some vendors may elect not to respond to the RFP based on the budget – that's perfectly acceptable.

## Review the Proposals

Be sure to document the date, time, and recipient for each RFP response. An acknowledgement e-mail to the vendor is acceptable practice, but use care in the wording to not create or imply acceptance of the proposal. Allow the peer review or advisory group to review the submissions. Establish an objective rating system.

Stay focused on the requirements established by the needs document and the RFP, not on marketing tools or features the vendors promote. The training center, as the customer and user of the LMS, is the sole arbiter of what is or is not important. The review team should also keep an open mind. In almost every review of submitted proposals, at least one or more overlooked idea or requirement turns up.

Not every situation is clear-cut. If a vendor RFP fails to show how a critical requirement will be met, the tendency is to eliminate the vendor from contention. Depending on other vendor responses, it may be appropriate to keep a vendor in contention even though they are missing a core capability. If the vendor presents an acceptable alternative or can fulfill the need through customization, the best course might be to keep the vendor in the running.

As responses are evaluated, consider responses to requirements when viewed as part of the project plan or timeline:

- High-priority requirements should be able to be met at the time of implementation.
- Medium-priority requirements may not be met during the initial implementation, but compliance and time frame should be part of the project plan.
- Low-priority requirements, or "nice to have" features can be referenced more vaguely. Depending on the vendor's response, these lower-priority items can possibly be escalated in priority, or deleted altogether.

With virtually every vendor's submission, there should be gaps between the vendor response and the LMS specification document.

---

**No single LMS will fully meet a training center's needs immediately upon implementation.  Be wary of ANY vendor claiming to do so.**

---

Gaps between the vendor's existing product and the training center's needs are the reason the customization line item should be in the budget.  When a gap is identified, talk with the vendor about how the system adapts to such customizations or extensions. *Customizations* refer to changeable parameters within the confines of the system as it exists when sold.  *Extensions* refer to functions or features not found in the software, but added by the vendor.  *Extensions* also refer to plug-ins or web services that allow the LMS to integrate or interface with other systems.

One unique consideration as submissions are evaluated is "build or buy".  Larger corporations, especially those with significant information technology resources, often consider building a learning management system because the training center's needs appear unique. Even though an "off-the-shelf" system may not have every function or feature deemed critical, it is often cheaper to have the selected vendor customize or extend an existing product than develop a solution internally.

---

**If a suitable vendor cannot be located in the first round of RFP's review the requirements and repeat the process with a new vendor pool.**

---

Narrow the submissions down to a "short list" of three vendors that meet critical requirements, including budget.  Getting to this point in the process allows the training manager to spend more time exploring needs with well-qualified vendors, rather than a small amount of time with a large number of vendors.  One LMS vendor is known to ask two screening questions before committing sales staff for demos and extended conversations with a potential new client: is there a clearly defined budget approved, and how many LMS vendors are currently being considered. While these questions may seem harsh, they provide valuable insight into where the training manager is at in the search for a learning management system.

### Schedule Meetings and Demos

Once a "short list" of three vendors is identified, develop a list of follow-up questions for each vendor. Schedule meetings between key personnel and the vendor; include others in a product demonstration if appropriate.

A vendor's demonstration of the system is often the first opportunity to see a product in service. Many vendors have a scripted demonstration they prefer to follow, often focusing on product strengths or high-profile features and minimizing weaknesses. Allow the vendor some latitude to conduct a scripted demonstration. The vendor may expose a feature or area of the product that has value to the training center. The scripted demonstration should not take more than 25 percent of the allotted time.

When approaching a vendor and requesting a demonstration:

- Prepare a list of questions related to specific features or processes that came up during the review of submitted RFPs. If any process or feature is unclear, ask the vendor to include it in the demonstration.
- If the LMS will be used for online course delivery, provide a content sample and ask that it be included in the demonstration. **
- Establish a "Top 10" list of the training center's most common LMS-related tasks and ask the vendor to demonstrate each (for example, create a course). Unlike widely varying scripted demos, having each vendor perform specific tasks allows a training center to compare a specific process among multiple platforms. **
- Ask the vendor to record the demonstration and make the recording available to members of the review group. Doing so can eliminate the need for the vendor to perform multiple demonstrations.
- Ask the vendor for access to a sample or demonstration site for a period of 5-7 days. Look at the processes used to perform common tasks and be sure the proposed solution supports the learning strategy and methods.

** The content sample and task list should be provided to each vendor doing a demonstration. Ensure vendors have enough lead time to answer questions and prepare for the meeting.

The demonstration component of the selection process is crucial in determining how compatible or flexible the vendor's environment is. The demo helps the training manager understand what functionality is included out-of-box versus elements that may require customization. Be sure to ask questions about any function or feature that is not clearly understood. The vendor should be able to explain functionality clearly and without ambiguity.

Completing the meeting and demonstration process narrows the list down to a leading contender. Involve stakeholders. Ask both objective (does it meet the training center's need?) and a subjective questions (is the vendor reputable and likeable?). Although the objective evaluation is very important, the training manager will be working closely with the LMS vendor. Building a friendly, professional relationship with the vendor pays dividends over the long term.

### Make the Selection

After all the research and demonstrations, and probably more than a few conference calls or meetings, the training organization can make a selection. The purchase of a learning management system is a serious, long-term investment. Although obtaining a unanimous agreement on the selection may be difficult, every stakeholder should feel that he or she had a role in the selection.

When all stakeholders have participated in the selection process and feel that their opinion has been respected, the implementation process is much easier. The more people that feel that they have contributed to the system, the more people will be championing the system when it is implemented.

The training manager should have a contingency plan. Unfortunately, cases do arise where a vendor or a product simply isn't a good fit for the organization. Throughout the implementation process, continue updating contingency plans. Problems can be as simple as a particular feature not meeting a specific requirement or more complex, such as the implementation falling behind schedule.

Just like with a training program, always have a backup plan and a backup to the backup plan. There is no substitute for planning when implementing a training or learning management system.

## Working with a LMS Vendor

Managing the relationship with the learning management system vendor largely falls to the training manager. Three basic steps can dramatically improve the relationship with the training center's vendor.

### 1. Understand Expectations

Customer satisfaction is defined as a measure of how a product or services supplied by a vendor compares to the customer's expectations. A good example of how expectations are defined? Hearing the familiar "Oh, yeahhhh..." from the iconic 80's movie *Ferris Bueller's Day Off*, then seeing the main character "in role" with a similar opening sequence. How did viewers react to the clip being a commercial for an automobile company? Understanding expectations and how they are formed is a big element of customer satisfaction. There are four basic sources for expectations: explicit promises, implicit promises, word-of-mouth communications and past experiences.

## Explicit Promises

Promises the LMS Vendor make to a training center are called explicit promises; these can come from sales documents, advertisements, articles, et cetera. This is the only area of customer expectations that a vendor actually controls. Explicit promises made by the vendor have a direct impact on what is expected during the relationship.

## Implicit Promises

Implicit promises are formed based on forces other than what is said by the vendor. Things like price perceptions (the higher the price, the better the service) and environmental perceptions (the vendor has 20 staff members for support) often form an expectation. Implicit promises based on perception can be a stumbling block; rely on facts and explicit promises.

## Word-of-Mouth

Statements that are perceived as unbiased or unsolicited, especially those appearing in the LMS vendor's support message board, can play a role. Customers expect the same level of service and support that they see being provided to other customers. As with implicit promises, every customer is different. Many LMS vendors have different support tiers and plans, with cost directly equality to the speed and availability of support.

## Past Experiences

Experiences with past LMS vendors can have a very strong effect on what is expected from current and future vendors. Even experiences with an internal IT department help desk can affect what is expected from the LMS vendor.

For more information on customer expectations of service, consider reviewing:
http://highered.mcgraw-hil.com/sites/dl/free/0077107950/577210/01ch03.pdf

## 2. Understand the Difference between Support and Help

LMS Vendors provide a complex software application that performs specific tasks. In most applications, the tasks that a learning management system will perform are well documented. Information on the functions of the LMS can be found in:

- Help files or documentation
- Forums
- Knowledge base articles
- Training

An LMS vendor considers it support when a function, feature, or service of the application does not work as it was designed or implemented. Examples of true support issues are:

- A hosted web site is down
- An error page displays after pressing a function button
- Making a change to single data element, and all the records are affected

*Help*

Many of the requests made to LMS vendors actually fall into a separate category – help. Help is best defined as when a client needs assistance using a function, feature or service of the application. Many help cases start with letting the vendor know what needs to be accomplished. Examples of help issues are:

- The wrong registration document is being emailed to students
- A user has access to data or functions he or she shouldn't have
- Deleting an incorrect record

Sometimes, a problem may not be easily identified as support or help, or may be a combination of both.

## 3. Manage Mutual Expectations

Learning management system installations are complex in part because of the number of users that they reach. Almost every user is accessing the system through a different computer, potentially from a different network, using different browsers, plug-ins, and so on. Even the largest LMS vendors cannot test against every possible configuration an end-user may have. The LMS vendor should have created a stable framework that functions well across a large user base. Ultimately, is the vendor responsible for the fact that someone failed to download the latest media player plug-in needed to view content created by the training designer? No. Does the vendor have a responsibility to provide help to that user? Maybe – depending on the expectations that have been defined.

The best advice for ensuring vendor expectations are met – be clear with the vendor. Likewise, the vendor should be clear about what will be provided, and live up to any guarantees or explicit promises made.

### Help Yourself

One function that can be easily implemented is the "training help desk". Establish an e-mail account and telephone number (it can even be voicemail-only) specific to problems within the training center. Identify a member of the training staff to be responsible for checking the account on a set schedule. Establish single points-of-contact between the vendor and the training center. Funnel all questions and help or support issues through these individuals. Help the vendor out by prioritizing issues if there are more than one.

Make use of the vendor's support web site or portal to report bugs and request features. LMS vendors need feedback and ideas to improve their product.

### The LMS Vendor, Support, and Help

One of the most common problems that a LMS vendor encounters with a client often happens early during the relationship. LMS vendors typically encourage potential clients to have a detailed requirements and technical implementation document. Having a detailed document at the outset helps manage expectations during the initial implementation, and ensures the application will handle all critical tasks. When a customer realizes that a feature is not available, or that is available but wasn't purchased – it is equally frustrating for everyone. The more detailed the initial requirements documents, the lower the likelihood of missing a needed feature.

LMS vendors want satisfied, happy customers. By communicating clearly and having defined expectations, training managers can get all the help and support needed and the LMS vendor can be a better partner.

## Making Money with a LMS

Many training centers view the monthly or annual payment to their learning management system vendor as a pure expense. The truth is a learning management system is an extremely valuable asset. In order to understand the measurable value of a learning management system, perceptions about training may need to change.

### 1. Training is Never Free.

Just because a training center doesn't charge participants or their business units an actual "price" to attend a class doesn't mean the training is free. "No Charge" simply means the training center isn't recovering the cost of training. Training centers need to break the paradigm that they are simply an expense category.

The training department is rarely a consumer of the training it produces or conducts – other business units are. The training center is more accurately a custodian of corporate funds, charged with using and dispersing funds in ways that improve the company's bottom line. The learning management system should be keeping up with three basic financial elements:

1. The cost of training,
2. Any revenue generated, and
3. The value of training.

A learning management system should be able to produce evidence of the following basic formula:

---

**Revenue + Value ≥ Cost**

---

Even though every class offered is "No Charge", the training center is making money for the company.

## 2. Market Training Activity.

People can't take training classes they don't know about. A learning management system is a significant piece of the marketing platform for any training center. If training programs require annual renewal or recertification, the LMS should be sending automatic reminders to those who need renewals.

Let students know about new or updated training programs. Use the LMS to deliver an e-mail study guide to students preparing for a certification exam. The ability to deliver specific, customized communications directly to a student helps build both personal and professional value.

A learning management system is the ultimate target marketing tool – make use of it.

## 3. Stop the Printing.

Printing and mailing information is one of the most expensive processes a training center can undertake. The data contained within the LMS allows a training center to utilize e-mail for marketing many training opportunities, in lieu of newsletters and mailings. A learning management system can provide the same type of high-quality certificate being printed – only the certificate can be delivered online or by e-mail. Many learning management systems allow self-service printing by the student.

### Case Study: Certificate Printing

A training center taught 60 classes of 20 students each year, printing and mailing 1200 certificates.

| | |
|---|---|
| Printing full-color certificates @ $1.50 each | $ 1,800.00 |
| Manila envelopes , 9" x 12", $0.10 each | $   120.00 |
| Postage, 1st class @ $ 1.30 each | $ 1,560.00 |
| Labor Cost, $10 / Hr., 10 Min. per Certificate | $ 2,000.00 |
| **Total Cost** | **$ 5,480.00** |

The staff member assigned to the task spent an average ten minutes per certificate getting them printed, addressed, put in envelopes, and mailed. Certificates accounted for 200 hours of work – almost 10 percent of the full-time employee's available work hours in the year. The training center virtually eliminated postage costs from the budget once the LMS was used to deliver training certificates, and the employee's time was much better utilized.

There are a number of other printed items that can potentially be replaced through use of the learning management system. Instead of printing a copy of the latest training metrics report, save it as a PDF file and e-mail the document to the management team.

With the cost of paper and printing consumables on the rise, every sheet of paper or toner cartridge conserved is a direct improvement of the company's bottom line.

## 4. Communicate.

Miscommunication costs time and productivity, especially in a corporate training environment.  Everyone needs to be informed of class date, time, or location changes.  Training managers should be able to easily identify and resolve scheduling or resource conflicts.

The learning management system should automatically inform the correct person when certain changes are made.  Using automated communications also helps avoid the proverbial "I didn't know!"  Little things like sending an appointment reminder that can be inserted directly into a student's mobile device or personal information manager can make a huge difference.

The goal is to use the learning management system to both prevent miscommunication and communicate change. In doing so, efficiency is increased and the impact of training on production and revenue is minimized.

## The LMS is not an Enemy

Don't look at a learning management system as an expense, or the enemy. A learning management system is a tool.  When used to track return on investment, market training and activity, and gain efficiency the LMS can be one of the most profitable elements of a training center.

# WORKS CITED

Dassault Systems, SA v. Childress, 10-1987 (United States Court of Appeals, 6th Circuit December 13, 2011).

American Society for Training & Development. (2011, December 5). *2008 Industry Report: Gauges & Drivers*. Retrieved from American Society for Training & Development: http://www.astd.org/

Anovick, P. (2010, July 12). *Simple Steps for Tactful Communication*. Retrieved from @rticles: http://ezinearticles.com/?Simple-Steps-For-Tactful-Communication&id=4651141

Barbouletos, S. M. (2011). *Discrepancy Between Role Expectations and Job Descriptions: The Impact on Stress and Job Satisfaction*. Bothell, WA: University of Washngton - Bothell.

Cutting, T. (2006, December 8). *Scope Creep, Part 2*. Retrieved from Cutting's Edge Project Management: http://cuttingsedgepm.blogspot.com/2006/12/december-8-2006-scope-creep-part-2.html/

Dale, E. (1969). *Audiovisual Methods in Teaching, 3rd Ed.* Dryden Press.

Doll, S. (2001, March 13). *Seven Steps for Avoiding Scope Creep*. Retrieved from TechRepublic: http://www.techrepublic.com/article/seven-steps-for-avoiding-scope-creep/1045555?tag=ccontent;siu-container

FIA Institute for Motor Sport Safety and Sustainability. (2012). *Officials Safety Training Program Best Practices Framework*. Paris, France: FIA Institute for Motor Sport Safety and Sustainability.

Highet, G. (1989). *The Art of Teaching*. New York, NY: Vintage Books.

Lucas, S. E. (2009). *The Art of Public Speaking, 10th Edition*. New York, NY: McGraw-Hill.

Mager, R. F. (1996). Morphing into a 21st Century Trainer. *Training*, 47-50, 52-54.

Meister, J. C. (2000, June). The CEO-Drive Learning Culture. *Trainnig + Development*, pp. 52-58.

Noe, R. A. (2010). *Employee Training and Development.* New York, NY: McGraw-Hill Irwin.

Norton, A. (2010, July 27). *10 things that define a true professional.* Retrieved from TechRepublic: http://www.techrepublic.com/blog/10things/10-things-that-define-a-true-professional/1685

Stanford University. (2012, November 1). *Fair Use.* Retrieved from Stanford University: http://fairuse.stanford.edu/

Tallahassee Community College. (2012, August 28). *Learning Outcomes.* Retrieved from Tallahassee Community College: http://content.tcc.fl.edu/cte/Activity1/learning_outcomes_print.html

Thalheimer, W. (2006, October 8). *People remember 10%, 20%...Oh Really?* Retrieved from Will at Work Learning: http://www.willatworklearning.com/2006/10/people_remember.html

Thalheimer, W. (2009, January 13). *Myths the Business Side has About Learning.* Retrieved from Will at Work Learning: http://www.willatworklearning.com/2009/01/myths-the-business-side-has-about-learning-result-of-data-gathering.html

Thalheimer, W. (2011, November 22). *Is Your Training Course Likely to Boost Performance?* Retrieved from Will at Work Learning: http://www.willatworklearning.com/2011/11/free-course-review-template.html

Wideman, M. (2012, December 5). *Wideman Comparative Glossary of Project Management Terms.* Retrieved from Max's Project Management Wisdom: http://maxwideman.com/pmglossary/PMG_S01.htm